A Brown I

CW00458293

Album

Mr Reg Clements at Old Woodhouse Farm 1950s. The farm was 52 acres and Reg farmed it for 30 years from about 1940. Before Old Woodhouse Reg lived at Coppice Farm, Hill Top. He later re-married and moved to Rhyl with his new wife, Edith. He became the verger at St Thomas' Church in Rhyl. He died at the age of 87.

Compiled by Elizabeth Lawton
and Rosamond Unwin

Front cover:
June Willot & Ann Morris lead Queen Doris Moss out of St Anne's Church, 1946.

Back cover:
Exterior of the Hesketh Engine House July 1989.
School Bank (c.1950), four houses built by local builder James Simcock in 1912.

NAMES IN ALL CAPTIONS ARE LISTED LEFT TO RIGHT.

CHURNET VALLEY BOOKS
1 King Street, Leek, Staffordshire. ST13 5NW 01538 399033 www.leekbooks.co.uk
© Elizabeth Lawton, Ros Unwin and Churnet Valley Books 2009 ISBN 9781904546696

Ros

A big thank you to everyone who contributed photographs and shared memories with us. Thanks also to those who helped with the Heaton research; Phil Durber's knowledge was invaluable as was that given by two Heaton gentlemen (Matthew from Birmingham and John from Cheshire) who, although not connected with the Brown Edge Heatons, went out of their way to help track down the pictures on page 22. If anyone knows of any pictures of the Heaton ladies (Mary, Kate and Lydia) or Poole Fields we'd love to see them.

I hope you'll forgive any errors - we've done our best. Finally, I'd like to thank Elizabeth for all her kindness and for inviting me to do this in the first place. It has been quite an experience!

CONTRIBUTORS:

Deanna Durber
Bob Durber
Jean and Dennis Holdcroft
Bob Chadwick
Edward and Marjorie Selby
Doris Moss
Norah and John Garner
Dave Scarlett
The Endonian Society
Graham and Ann Mitchell
Marjorie Foster
Pauline Higginbotham
Peter Lowe
Margaret Ball
Chris Tatton
Irene Cartlidge
John & Paul Chadwick
Judith Hodgkinson
Alan Hayes
Nancy Bell
Alan Pointon
Yvonne Hargreaves
Stan & Dave Davenport
Christine Tate

Valerie McGrath
David Leese
Caroline Durber
John Triner
John Bourne
Ray Adams
Philip Durber
Stephen Myers, Helen Mason, Myers & Co
Mike Skerratt
Paul Carrol
Wendy Scragg
Pat Carter
Hilda Simcock
Shirley Hudson
Gwenyth Salt
Derith Proctor
Barbara Atkins
Eric Hargreaves
Elsie Rowland
Flo Adderley
Beryl Hulstone
Lorna Lovatt
Dorothy & Brian Simcock
Joan Mountford

Elsie Thompson
Lewis Pointon
Diane and Carl Machin

Others who helped: Pat Hull, Nigel Upright, Pete Meadowcroft, Betty Mosedale, Sid Boulton, Peter Fynn, Brenda Stanway, Geoff Browne at Leek Post and Times, the staff at Staffs Record Office and Hanley Library.

John Fenton
Elizabeth Charles
Reg Twemlow
Robert & David Willis
Jean Mayer
Belle Lovatt
Sandra Hancox
Gladys Bailey
Betty Lowe
Susan Williams
Paul Dickinson
Irene Daniels
Norman Hughes
Dave Harvey

A view over St Anne's Vale with Dawson's house and garden in the foreground in the 1950s.
This house has been rebuilt and is now part of Ash Tree Farm.

Elizabeth

I thought *Brown Edge 2* would be my last book but then I met Ros Unwin, we became friends and her enthusiasm led to *A Brown Edge Album*. I had some unpublished photos left and Ros had some, and once again we had an amazing response from Brown Edgers. The book was just going to be photos but then we felt we had to include the stories we were told. We wanted to include all the photos we saw but soon realised it was impossible when relying on memory. I would like to thank Ros and all those who have contributed photos and just hope this book gives as much pleasure as I had in compiling it.

Thanks also to Clive & Sheila Proctor, Fred & Mavis Snape, Brian & Louise Chadwick, and Ken Bedson.

Camping with Endon School. John Tatton far right.

Scout tea at the school, late 1950s. Back: ?, ?. George Hall, Albert Nixon, ?, John Fenton
2nd Row: Mrs Carroll, Robert Willis, ?, Peter Worthy, Stuart Beardmore, Gerard Carroll, Robert Charlesworth, Mrs Fenton.
Front: David Willis, Jan Bakowski, John Tyler, Paul Carroll, John Simmonds, Noel Carroll, George Zurek, Graham Abbott.

A BROWN EDGE CHILDHOOD · JOHN BOURNE

I was born at my grandma's house in Norton at the end of the war in 1942. We lived at Rock House, The Rocks, Brown Edge. The house was owned by Harry Hammond and the rent was ten shillings a week. It was an exciting place to live for a youngster; we had rocks to climb in the Stone hole and a wooded drive with bushes to hide in and trees to climb. At the back we had a small heather moor where we caught butterflies and bees which we kept in jam jars.

My father, also John Bourne but always known as Jack, worked in the pit and our load of coal was always tipped at the end of our long drive. My brother Dennis and myself had to wheelbarrow the ton of coal down the drive and stack it in the coal shed. Winters then were harsh, always heavy snow and well below freezing. It always froze our water pipes and we had to draw water from the well in our front garden. We enjoyed the snow, particularly sledging down the extremely steep Slater's Field in St Anne's Vale. The sledges were handmade, usually by your father, with metal runners and were very heavy to pull back up the hill. Sliding in the school playground was also popular - we added nails to the soles of our boots to make them slide better.

Rock House was quite a way from the shops but my mother Vera used to send me so often to the Co op, I can still remember the divi number - 13111. Bread, butter, sugar, jam from the Co op and call at Les Harrison's Butchers for a leg of lamb (we were a big family), and a trip to Jolley's shop at Lane Ends for cough mixture, all in one morning. I was a good friend of Graham Mitchell and spent many summer evenings playing football in the fields outside the bungalow with his dad Tom keeping goal. Shufflebottom's Farm (as we knew it), Singlet House Farm, was across the road from Graham's bungalow and we used to go there to help milk the cows by hand. Roy Woodward, another mate, lived nearby in Back Lane. His family was one of the first in Brown Edge to have a TV and Roy used to invite all his mates in to view the 9" black and white. Ivor Jones' family also had a TV and I remember enjoying every match of the 1950 World Cup there.

The end of September was the conker season. Malcolm Sims and myself knew every good conker tree in Brown Edge, Endon and Norton Green and would walk miles and spend hours throwing sticks to knock off the conkers. We would bake them in the oven to make them really hard. We would play before school, during breaks, lunchtime and after school, great sport. During the summer holidays we would go to Knypersley fishing with a net made from one of my mother's old nylon stockings, a large jam jar to put the fish in, jam sandwiches and a bottle of water. We would bring home red penks, bullnoggers and sticklebacks, which we caught at the feeder river, the Trent and Knypersley Mill Pool. We would be gone all day and my mother would say *'I'm going to Hanley, I'll leave the catch on the latch'*. We also enjoyed making bow and arrows - a good straight holly branch I remember made the best bow.

Other great memories are playing cricket in the Stone hole with my brother Dennis, Frank Selby and Duncan Hall. Duncan had a proper treble sprung Gradidge bat that had once belonged to Stan Crump and a good corky cricket ball. We played for hours, the stumps were a pile of rocks. Also trips into the countryside with Malcolm Sims, an expert at bird nesting. He would take you to skylarks nests on Marshes Hill and curlews and lapwings on the fields between Brown Edge and Endon. Malcolm was a real country bumpkin, he used to tickle trout and bring home great crested newts, which we would keep for days in jam jars. He always knew where there was a plentiful supply of mushrooms and when watercress was in season.

Few people liked Phyllis Davenport our schoolteacher but Malcolm and myself enjoyed her lessons focusing on the countryside and farming. She once asked us to cut out pictures of Jersey cows from farming magazines, so many people had these in Brown Edge it was easy to obtain a copy. There were lessons on milk quality and quantity. The school once purchased a large quantity of bulbs and she asked us all to collect a bag of leaf mould to set them in, sending us to the local woods depending where we lived. I went to Tinster's Wood where there was plenty of really good quality.

Mr. Fisher the headmaster used to organize cricket matches after school, we played in the school playground. David Steele (later to play for England) was in our class and he was so good that eventually Mr. Fisher would have him playing the rest of the class and he would still win. We stopped playing when one of David's hook shots broke Mr Fisher's schoolhouse window. Cricket with David Steele in the Hollybush Fields was another great memory, I would bowl at him for hours not getting him out and then he would give me several innings.

My brother Dennis and myself were quite enterprising at an early age. Our family had always reared poultry and we used to purchase day old chicks which we would fatten up for Christmas and then kill, pluck and dress them before selling them to family and neighbours. Dennis later took to scrap metal collecting, stripping down old cookers and the like, it was quite profitable. Ever likely we did well in business together when we established our successful sports shop. Malcolm Sims lived in Rose Cottage, St Anne's Vale. He had a bike and his dad had a bike with Sturmy Archer gears which I borrowed. We used to cycle to Rudyard Lake, Alton Towers, the Wrekin and Queens Park, Crewe plus a really great ride with Malcolm and Colin Oakley to Matlock Bath.

Jack Sherratt the newsagent persuaded me to take on the Hill Top paper round. It was the least number of Sentinels, only 65, but some of the deliveries were a long way apart. Unwin's Farm on Marshes Hill and Foxes who lived at the far side of Marshes Hill were included in the round. Dennis used to help me and we would split the number of papers and race each other to the finish. Simcocks at Fiddlers Bank was the last paper and we would not stop running until we got back to the village.

In summer we would go haymaking. Mr Lowe from Pool House at Jobs Pool taught us how to use the pickle, hayfork and rake. We would work all day and the only reward would be a drink of lemonade or dandelion and burdock, which we would be pleased with. We also went potato picking for farmer Reg Clements at Woodhouse Lane Farm, picking the potatoes by hand, filling two buckets and walking the length of the field to empty the buckets into the horse cart - it was hard work and we worked all day for one shilling and sixpence.

On Friday nights we attended the youth club at the chapel in Sandy Lane, run by Arthur Berrisford. We also spent many nights at the YMCA (Tab) playing table tennis, snooker and billiards. Thursdays was Rock and Roll night at the Tab and Ivor Jones and myself never missed bopping with Edith Brereton (Bedson) and Joan Dawson, they came all the way from Ball Green. Some came from as far away as Leek.

I went to Endon High School until I was thirteen and I went to Leek High after passing my 13+ exam. Endon School was really enjoyable; we had a great PE master Bob Drummond. He took a great interest in cross-country and football. In the winter our school teams competed with schools from Leek, Alan Waterfall, who ran the Leek and District football team that played in the English Schools National competition and Leckie Shield, selected several Brown Edger's for the team. Graham Mitchell, David Steele,

A fine shot to leg from David Steele from Brown Edge, who at 18 played as club professional at Newcastle and Hartshill before he joined Northants. He made his debut for England aged 33 and scored a half century in his first innings.

Dennis with his scrap metal.

John, Malcolm Sims, Colin Oakley at Matlock Bath.

David Crossley and myself were in one team. I enjoyed running and track and field which Bob Drummond encouraged, Peter Baker was a good high jumper and Graham Mitchell was a really good javelin thrower. I was in the county championships with them.

My family eventually moved to keep a pub in Burslem, The Millstone. Our links with Brown Edge didn't end there. We employed Brian Oakes's band, Bry Martin and the Marauders, to play each week for a few years. When I started courting Eileen, who came from

Endon School Football Team 1954-55. Back: Graham Mitchell, Keith Snape, Ivor Jones, Geoff Randall, Roy Woodward, David Berrisford, ?, ? Daniels, Alan Trotter Seated John Bourne, Bob Drummond, David Steele, Sam Edwards, John Lee.

Stoke, we would travel by bus to Brown Edge and walk to Knypersley Pool. She fell in love with Brown Edge and we bought our first house, 1 Leonard Drive in the April that we were marrying in the September. The previous owner of the house was a Mr Garski; it had everything I had always dreamed of, a big vegetable garden and greenhouse. We shook hands on the deal for the house and I asked if he minded if I set some potatoes the next night in the garden because it was getting late in the season for sowing potatoes. When I went to the solicitors a few days later it was the talk of the office that I had potatoes set before I had signed the contract. Although I now live in Endon my runs, bike rides and walks to keep fit almost always involve Brown Edge and I still stop and talk to some of the old timers - many still refer to me as Jack Bourne's lad.

Endon School, Birchall Sports Ground c 1955. Back: ?, Peter Baker, Harold Lowe, ?, ?, John Bourne, ?, ? Front: Gordon Hansell, teacher Leek High School, ? Graham Mitchell in action.

St Anne's Vale c 1950 with Brookfield in the centre of the picture (the house where Mrs Benton lived). Prospect Villa can be seen on the far right.

The front entrance of Prospect Villa with Clara Weaver on the left and Lily Pointon right. The house was converted to two semi-detached houses in 1970.

Who are these characters?

Ash House - Harvey Durber
lived here from 1946.
He was born in 1915 at
Knypersley Mill Farm, the
second child of five born to
Arthur and Martha Durber
(nee Harvey). During his
childhood Harvey lived at The
Sands, Marshes Hill and Park
Lane in Knypersley and spent
much of his time with his
grandfather, William Durber,
at Singlet House Farm.
A well known local character,
Harvey could lift half a
hundredweight with his teeth!

JOB'S POOL

The 1840 Tithe Map shows that Job Bailey
erected a cottage with a small cow house
attached, which he named Appletree Farm.
As the nearest water was half a mile away
Job dammed a small stream, which flowed
down St Anne's Vale. This formed a small
pool in front of his cottage, for his cattle.
The pool has disappeared but this area is
still known as Job's Pool.

Durber's Cottage in Sandy Lane in the late 1930s with May Durber
(Lorna Lovatt's mother). The cottage is still there and is called Petra.

Ann Lowe aged 8 in the garden of Pool House, Job's Pool
with Apple Tree Farm in the background (Selby's cottage).

The official opening of the Playing Field, 15 April 1961.
Back: Lynn Foster, Irene Foster, Adrian Mickiewicz (Mason), ?, ?, ?, George Bond, ?, Harry Hammond.
Front: Alderman Hancock, Terry Slater, Sandra Beff, Sir Alfred Owen, Jack Heath, Colin Simcock.
Children: Christopher Beff, ?, Susan Adderley. The swings were later re-positioned.

Sir Alfred Owen, a Staffordshire industrialist, had previously that day laid the foundation stone to the new Sandy Lane chapel. The land for the playing field was purchased from the brewery company for £150.
Sir Alfred gave £100 for the erection of a pavilion.

```
          NORTON  PARISH  COUNCIL



            OFFICIAL  OPENING

               of the

        BROWN  EDGE  PLAYING  FIELD

                 on

        SATURDAY,  15th  APRIL,  1961.

                 by

        ALDERMAN  A. G. B. OWEN, C.B.E.,
     (Chairman of Staffordshire County Council)




        CHAIRMAN - ALDERMAN  W. HANCOCK
           (Chairman of Parish Council)
```

```
              P R O G R A M M E


         ASSEMBLE  OUTSIDE  ENTRANCE
         ----------
             UNLOCKING  OF  GATES
                   by
             COUNCILLOR  H. HAMMOND
         (Chairman of Playing Fields Committee)
             ------
         WELCOME  ADDRESS  TO  ALDERMAN  OWEN, C.B.E.,
                   by
             ALDERMAN  W. HANCOCK
             ------
             PRAYERS  OF  DEDICATION
                   by
             REV.  P. H. HANKS
             ------
         PROCESSION  TO  PLATFORM  FOR  OFFICIAL  OPENING
             ------
             EXPRESSION  OF  THANKS
                   by
             COUNCILLOR  J. HEATH
         (Vice Chairman Parish Council)
                  and
             COUNCILLOR  J. MARSHALL
             (Chairman  Leek R.D.C.)
             ----oOo----
```

Broad Lane Cottage 1967. Graham Hudson on left, Robert Hudson right. This was two cottages at the time. It was part of a smallholding that had been in the Willott family for a very long time (a map of 1814 shows Willott as the owner). The last of the family, Samuel Willott, died in 1954 and the land sold. George Unwin bought the cottages and two acres. Mr Harrison of Fernyhough Farm bought three fields in front, known as Brown Bank.

RIGHT:
Sandy Lane. Chedder Hargreaves centre with Frank Moss behind. In the background can be seen the old workingmen's club built on Scarlett's old garden.

BELOW:
Bluestone Farm c 1960 showing the cow house attached. The farm belonged to the Water Board and was demolished in the 1970s. Alan Marshall, David Simcock, Len Marshall, Brian Simcock, Alan Simcock, Joe Simcock, Ernest Johnson, Herbert Spinks.

An early view of Sandy Lane, the Hollybush pub on the left.
This part of Sandy Lane was later renamed High Lane.
There was a large garden at the side of the pub where the car park is
now. The 1851 census shows the licensee as Joseph Bullock, the
village butcher. Trade Directories show Joseph Dawson as the beer
retailer in 1876, Mr Francis Knowles in 1900, George Gunn in 1920
and Lee Burgess in 1940.
Mountford's Row on the right was built in 1876 by Mr Charles, a
local builder, for Mr Mountford - known as 'Turp'.

George Scarlett in Sandy Lane standing in his garden
(where the chapel is now). The New Inn is in the
background. The New Inn was used as the police house
for a while and was demolished about 1954.
A trade directory for 1880 lists Charles Frost as inn-keeper
and one for 1900 lists Enoch Pickford.

Horace and Lottie Hayes
behind the bar at the
Roebuck c 1958. Albert
Bickerton on the right used
to live in and look after
Tinster's Wood. Alan Hayes
remembers being chased
out of the wood by Albert
many times, and then
facing him in the pub at
night. The Roebuck closed
in mid-1970s and is now
Keith's Workshop.

Paul Dickinson: Major Dickinson

My grandfather, Major Charles Lampriere Herbert Dickinson had family connections with Rotherham and was one of three, two boys and a girl. He was married in 1905 to Maude Boddington whose family came from Porthill. When my grandparents were first married they lived at Endon, in the house that became the NatWest Bank. Grandfather was training to be a land agent and I believe had connections with Heaton's.

In the First World War he served with the Leicestershire Regiment and was wounded and lost the sight of one eye. He was awarded the DSO. The family moved to Brown Edge and lived in Tally-Ho Cottage. Grandfather loved to choose eccentric names for the children - I think my grandmother named the son just called Robert when Grandfather was away at war.

I do not know the date when they left Brown Edge. Grandfather retired to Droitwich and died in the mid 1950s and my grandmother died in about 1973.

An early view of Breach Road (The Avenue). Major Dickinson and his family lived in the house in foreground, Tally-ho Cottage. It later became a café.

Major Dickinson with his wife and eight children c 1918. L-R: Brenda Audrey Boddington Dickinson as May Queen on Hospital Saturday, Ethel Maude Boddington Dickinson (known as Edytha), Gerald Alwyn Roose Dickinson, Major Dickinson, Mrs Dickinson, Robert Dickinson, Darrell St Clair Davenport Dickinson (Jack), Hilda Patricia Boddington Dickinson (Biddie), Bertie Atherton Powys Dickinson, Dillon Guy Saville Dickinson.

Clem Hughes (the grandfather of Norman Hughes) who used to deliver beer to local pubs. He lived in Lion's Paw Wood in a wooden bungalow. He also started the canteen at Chatterley Whitfield Colliery.

The wooden bungalow near Lion's Paw Wood where Clem Hughes lived. Later, when Keith Fisher lived here the Marauders group used to practice there. It was destroyed by fire in the late 1950s.

Mr Beech from Lion's Paw Farm in Ladymoor Lane.

Herbert Hughes, (Norman's father) with his bell tent in Lion's Paw Wood in the later 1920s.

Chris Tatton: Ash Tree Farm

My parents, Lily and Dan Tatton, moved to Ash Tree Farm in 1947. The house had been a farmhouse dating back many years. The upstairs was reached by wooden steps more like a ladder and the end room upstairs had been a hayloft. There was only one cold-water tap and cooking was done on the range. Dan used to grow annual bedding plants and tomatoes in the two large glass houses. Tatton's tomatoes were a must for quite a few 'Brine Edgers' for Sunday tea on a summer's day. Lily and Dan were both members of the over 60's and Dan was president for about 7 years.

I was born in 1943 and went to St. Anne's School and then Endon School. I joined the Chatterley Whitfield Band in 1955 aged 12. I worked at Harrison's butchers and then Browns in Hanley. In 1965, I started at Valley Service Station at Norton Green and in 1975 became a sales rep selling motor parts. In 1982 I joined a group trying to re-open the derelict Theatre Royal in Hanley. In 1989 I took over as licensee of the theatre and Frank Roden and I became part of the Theatre Trust. For a short while we were joint owners. In 1994 my mother died and I had to retire from the theatre to look after my father. Dad died in 1997 and we decided to sell Ash Tree Farm. It was sold at auction on December 3rd 1998. We now live at Loggerheads and enjoy lots of holidays.

Ash Tree Farm. This smallholding was occupied in 1840 by John Sherratt Senr. and remained in the Sherratt family until the 1920s when Obediah Sherratt died.

BELOW: Chris backstage with Ken Dodd at the Theatre Royal 1989.

Chris outside Ash Tree Farm.

Lily and Dan Tatton. They had two sons, John and Chris. John married Joy Weaver and they had three children.

Lily with one of their pigs. Lily and Dan raised pigs for many years in the early 1960s.

Ash Tree Farm. Lily and Dan with son Chris in front of the ash tree, early 1960s.

PC Reginald Twemlow

I was born in 1920 at Sandford Hill. When I left school aged fourteen I worked in the Blacksmith's shop at Moss Field Colliery. In 1940 I joined the Irish Guards. I was demobbed in 1946. I married Marjorie Brennan in 1947 and joined the Staffordshire Police in 1948. I came to Brown Edge in 1953 and stayed about 10 years. I went into the Motor Division at Leek until my retirement in 1973.

One of the saddest times was when I went as part of a mobile unit to help at the Aberfan disaster. One of the best things I remember at Brown Edge was seeing Philip Rushton start his police career and end as Chief Superintendent.

Rosslyn, the old police station at corner of High Lane and Willfield Lane. George Scarlett, left and Jim Scarlett. The village constable in 1900 is recorded as PC Lycett. PC Staples followed and when he retired in 1919 the house was still the police house. PC Ibbs came in 1920 and lived in the old New Inn in Sandy Lane, as did PC Rowe. This building then became the police station. When PC James came in 1934 the station was transferred to one of the new houses in High Lane built by Mr. Enoch Dawson. PC Twemlow moved to the village in 1953, after the sudden death of PC Evans. S.C.C. built a new police house on land at the corner of Brownhills Road and Sytch Road and PC Twemlow was the first person to occupy it, early 1950s.

Dave Scarlett c 1948 outside Rosslyn in High Lane. Turner's bus is in the background.

The Battle for Water

In 1952 Endon Fox and his sons, Joseph and Levi, hired the services of a water diviner to find water for their property at The Sands on Marshes Hill. They went down 63 foot and after two unsuccessful attempts they decided to put a charge between the two holes and found water. L-R: Vera Fox, the diviner Alan Brown, Joe Fox, Aggie Fox, Endon Fox, Levi Fox and the shot-blaster, Wilf Simcock. Cynthia Shufflebottom is the little girl at the front.

In 1937 the residents of Hill Top still had no mains water supply and so they formed a committee and approached the two parish councils, the MP and Leek RDC (*Weekly Sentinel*) *'For months the RDC debated the question and finally Mr Ralph Charlesworth wrote to Sir Kingsley Wood, the then Minister of Health. Later he wrote again for in the meantime the council had decided to dispense with further discussion on the matter. Knowing that Sir Kingsley was a Methodist local preacher Mr Charlesworth appealed to his Christian sense of duty. It had a definite result for an inquiry was held.'*

Mr Charlesworth told the inquiry that there was only one tap to serve 86 people who lived in the 18 houses in Chapel Lane. Sometimes the tap did not run at full force and people had to go several times a day (The stand tap up New Lane). They also used the wells and springs, which sometimes dried up in the summer. When Mr Charlesworth finished there was a big outburst of applause but the Inspector said, *'We can cut out the applause. It does not cut any ice with me.'* As the inquiry came to a close a woman shouted *'How would you like to carry 27 buckets of water up a hill on washing day?'* Mr Charlesworth later showed the Inspector the stand tap and wells. A week passed then came notice that water had to be laid on in the area immediately.

91 years old Mr George Boulton and his 84 year old wife, Charlotte, have just had running water installed but they still enjoy a daily glass of spring water. *'The taste is different'* said Mrs Boulton. *'This tap water tastes artificial. It's full of chemicals'.* *(Leek Post & Times 1966)*

Jack and Jill still fetch water (Leek Post & Times 1966) 81 years old Joseph Horne and his wife Alice carry spring water back to their house. The majority of houses now have piped water but Mr Horne and his wife still fetch spring water. *'We have been using the spring for 35 years, and I feel healthier for it. Piped water just wouldn't be the same.'*

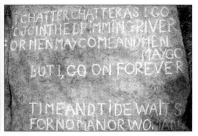

These stones around Hill Top were carved by Jacker Berrisford. He lived at Stanley View (formerly Collier's Arms) and was a well-known local character. He died in 2003. Stones cleaned and photographed by Jim Ryles.

St Anne's Vale. The Tab can be seen on the right. The cottages centre are Holmlea and Rock View. Dorothy Rushton, Alma Proctor and Gladys Bailey c 1939.

The Tab (short for Tabernacle)

The first YMCA building was erected in 1905 on School Bank opposite the school. It was replaced by a wooden building in 1929 and repositioned to St Anne's Vale. The old wooden building was replaced again in 1953 with a more substantial ex-army camp brick structure. A team of local men erected the hut, which was completed and re-opened in 1955. The Tab was used extensively for sport and social activities. The Thursday night dances are fondly remembered, when teenagers came from all around to have a good jive at the Tab. It was demolished in 1988 and a bungalow erected on the site.

LEFT & BELOW
Brown Edge YMCA Annual Dinner Dance
and Presentation June 2nd 1956.

The Grace

BY REV. W. ATTOE
PRESIDENT Y. M. C. A.

Menu

SOUP
TONGUE & CHICKEN
STUFFING, SALAD
TRIFLE
CHEESE & BISCUITS
COFFEE.

WELCOME
By Chairman ALDERMAN W. HANCOCK

PRESENTATION OF CHEQUE
To MR. NORTH by MR. J. BENTON
on behalf of the Y. M. C. A.

PRESENTATION OF TROPHIES
To the Y M C. A. Football Team
By MR. H. HAYNES Secretary
Leek & Moorland League
Introduced by MR. J. RUSHTON Chairman
of Y. M. C. A. Football Club

VOTE OF THANKS
By MR. C. SIMCOCK

DANCING
M. C. MR. A. SHERRATT

21st birthday of June Heath (nee Willett) in the Tab, late 1950s. Stewart Ball on Hawaiian guitar, left Selwyn Knight, right Charlie ?.

John Chadwick The Cross

I didn't know the cross was there at first - you wouldn't know unless somebody showed you. When I was 9 or 10 I used to walk up the path with my grandfather, James Chadwick when we took papers to Rock Cottage. Grandad used to say to me *'Look at that cross there, John'* - you could just make it out as it was covered in moss. It was built into the old wall, it was about 2 foot and like a Celtic cross. The wall went up in steps and they reckon that's where they used to put candles.

Slater's drive used to come up and go round a very sharp bend to Rock Cottage and opposite the house was this massive pear tree - all the old lads, Fred Proctor and that remember it because they've all gone pinching pears. Old Simcock used to come out with a stick and run us.

Grandfather said when he was a lad, when you came round this bend there used to be an archway, and a wall where they've put the gates now. All round the trees there used to be these stones in half circles. A man from Archives in Stafford said it probably went back to the time of Henry VIII and the Reformation. It was a place of prayer and they used it to baptize the babies. There were some big square stones for sitting on and one stone hollowed out. I think they used that as a font.

One day Grandfather was surprised to find the cross was all cleaned up. He thought he was the only one who knew where it was and the next thing it had gone - all the square stones went as well. There's no trace of it now. The old wall was knocked down in the early 1940s. Is this where Cross Edge got its name?

Youngsters at the back of the miners' houses 1982.
Back: Fay Worrall, Julie Snape holding Andrew Snape, ?, ?, ?Kapusta, ?.
Front: Darren Snape, Vonla Timms, ?, Brian Worrall, Alan Worrall, Johnny Berrisford, Terry Allen, Kevin Snape, Pamela Snape.

In 1956 the National Coal Board bought land on both sides of Breach Road to build houses for its employees. Workers came from all over the country to work in the North Staffordshire coalfields. The land was formerly part of the Heaton Estate. Building commenced in early 1957. 100 houses were built.

Elizabeth Charles: Rock Cottage

Rock Cottage was built as a shooting lodge in 1846. It belonged to Abner Wedgwood who was born in 1813 and died there in 1869. He married Ann Taylor Heath and eventually became manager of the Caldon Canal. It was originally just a two storey stone house, two rooms up, two down. The lodge was extended in about 1900. There was a lovely garden with a summerhouse, stables and a coach house. It also had an icehouse.

The Turner and Slater family lived there from April 1893 to June 1942. Mr Slater was Director for Art at Doultons in Burslem. He did experimental pottery work in a small building in the grounds. In 1942 the house was bought by Enoch and Cicely Haughton.

My family bought the house in November 1943. My father, James Charles, was a pharmacist, as was his father before him. They had a shop in Queen Street, Burslem, and three of Dad's sisters lived over the shop. Dad lived at Ridgway with my mother Dorothy, her parents, Grandma and Grandad Eaton, and my brother David. The whole family moved to Rock Cottage. Dad's sisters Elizabeth Ellen, Jane and Mary Alice, all unmarried, had their own wing and sitting room.

Dad died in 1979 and we moved to Ladderedge. Mum died in 1988 aged 80. The house was bought by Mr Kenneth Greene and converted into a nursing home in 1983. It also has a day nursery run by Julian Greene, his son, and Julian's wife Dawn.

ABOVE:
An early photo of the coach house and stables at Rock Cottage with members of the Slater and Turner family. The small building with chimney right of the stables was used by Mr Slater for experimental pottery work.

A family group at Rock Cottage. Elizabeth's christening 1944. Standing: Gertrude Pointon with Elizabeth, Dorothy Charles (mother), Elizabeth Ellen Charles (Nellie), Jane Charles (Jenny) and Mary Charles. Seated: Grandma Lizzie Eaton, David Charles, Grandpa Harry Eaton.

The original part of
Rock Cottage built in
1846 as a hunting lodge
for Abner Wedgwood

The black and white
extension was built in
about 1900.
The mound on the right
was the icehouse.

Elizabeth and David with their
parents Dorothy and James
Charles and Grandma Lizzie
Eaton, c 1945.

The front lawn looking down from the icehouse late 1950s. Auntie Jennie relaxing and David on the seat.

Ivy Cottage where Alfred Simcock and his family lived in the 1950s.

The garden after heavy snow in 1947.
L-R: Alfred Simcock, Elizabeth and Auntie Alice. The mound on the right of picture shows how deep the snow was.

POOLE FIELDS

Poole Fields, the home of the Heaton family for many years, was a detached house which stood where Poolfields Court is now. Richard Heaton, the founder of Heaton's solicitors, was born in 1820in Endon where his father was a Land Agent. Richard was living in Brown Edge when he married in 1854 and at Heaton Villas with his young family in 1861. By 1871 they had moved to Poole Fields.

We can't find any pictures of the house but Pat Hull (nee Price), who lived at a flat at Poole Fields in the 1950s and later in the bungalow in the grounds, remembers an impressive building (12 main rooms according to the 1911 census) which faced towards Endon. The iron gates by the roadside opened on to a curved, gravelled driveway leading to the front of the house. The cobbled tradesman's entrance further along the road led to the back of the house where there was a courtyard and several outbuildings. Behind these were an orchard and vegetable garden.

Heaton Villas were tenanted but No. 7 at the end of the row was used as the servants' living quarters; Elsie Pointon was one of the two live-in maids during the 1930s. The servants were expected to attend St Anne's Church every Sunday. Local people used to help at the house too - John Chadwick remembers his mum doing the family's laundry. As a boy he would deliver Mr Heaton's shirts and starched collars back to the house every Monday by the tradesman's entrance. His mother was paid five shillings for six shirts and 25 collars. Harry Pointon (Lewis Pointon's dad) collected the rents for the estate.

The Heaton land extended over the whole of the Cross Edge and Miners' Houses area to Willfield Lane. There was access to the grounds of the house from Occupation Road or Piggy Lane as we know it. Backing on to Piggy Lane were stables, cowsheds and a stockyard. Near to the end of the lane was a pool. John Chadwick remembers two other pools - one where Greenfield Place is now and the other near to the main road between Rock Cottage and Poolfields Court. The Davenport family were the tenants of Poole Fields Farm for many years.

Richard's son, Charles, qualified as a solicitor in 1880 and worked in the family business in Burslem where his sister, Lydia, was a typist. Nigel Upright (senior partner at Heatons until 2003) remembers being told by Harold Morton, Charles Heaton's partner, about an incident involving Charles and Harold Hales. Hales was the Burslem businessman said to be the inspiration for Arnold Bennett's 'Denry Machin' in *The Card*. He was at Heaton's office one day and had a disagreement with Charles. The argument became very heated and ended with Charles ejecting him from the office with the words *'Never darken this door again!'* Charles died in 1940 at his home in Hamil Road, Burslem. He had been Registrar of the Burslem County Court until he was 75. His son, Richard, became the third generation Heaton to work as a solicitor in the family business. The firm, which later became Heaton, Morton and Ryder, is now Heatons Solicitors based in Manchester but there is no longer a family connection.

Richard Heaton 1820-83   Charles Deane Heaton 1857-1940   Richard Heaton 1887-1958

Poole Fields School

Mary and Kate Heaton ran a private school from Poole Fields for many years. In the 1881 census Mary (21) and Kate (16) are living with their parents at Poole Fields. Both girls have 'at home' written beside their names where they were required to write their occupation. Their father died in 1883 and by the 1891 census Mary is a 'Music Teacher' and Kate a 'Private School Teacher'.

The school was listed as a day school in Kelly's Directory 1900. In 1901 they had one pupil boarding but in the years that followed they had quite a few from places like Birmingham and Derbyshire. There were a number

of local day pupils: Lily Dawson from Dawson's shop, the Phillips children from Willfield lane, Bessie Williamson from Endon, Edith Handley from Ridgeway Hall Farm, Arthur Lowe, and Charles Glass, the doctor's son. Charles followed in his father's footsteps and became the local doctor.

Philip Durber attended Poole Fields for a while and he has kindly let us include a couple of documents from his days there. He also has handwritten invoices from Kate Heaton showing the basic fee of two pounds two shillings per term with extras eg a 'Welcome Reader' is threepence, History is one shilling and

L-R Pat Price, Roy Berrisford, Doris Moss and Denise Price in front of what was the old schoolroom at Poole Fields.

Philip Durber's school report from the winter term 1931

an exercise book is threepence. When Philip was there the schoolroom was a wooden building in the grounds of the house; it was later converted into a bungalow and rented out. The Price family lived there for a while.

The family's association with Brown Edge ended when the last of the sisters Lydia died in 1946 aged 80. *The Leek Post and Times* reported that she was *'a member of an old and respected Brown Edge family'* and that she had had a long and valued association with St Anne's church. At one time she held meetings for the Church Bible Society at her home. She is buried in the family grave at St Anne's.

Shortly after Lydia Heaton's death the estate was split up and sold. Mrs Kate Sant bought the house and lived there until the 1950s. Later the house was used as the Workingmen's Club and subsequently demolished.

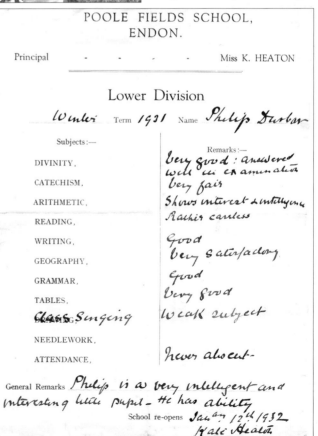

POOLE FIELDS SCHOOL,
ENDON.

Principal - - - - Miss K. HEATON

Lower Division

Winter Term *1931* Name *Philip Durber*

Subjects:— Remarks:—

DIVINITY, *very good: answered well in examination*

CATECHISM, *very fair*

ARITHMETIC, *Shows interest & intelligence*

READING, *Rather careless*

WRITING, *Good*

GEOGRAPHY, *very satisfactory*

GRAMMAR, *Good*

TABLES, *very good*

~~DRAWING~~ Singing *weak subject*

NEEDLEWORK,

ATTENDANCE, *Never absent*

General Remarks *Philip is a very intelligent and interesting little pupil- He has ability*

School re-opens *Jany 12th 1932*

Kate Heaton

A letter from Kate Heaton to Philip Durber's mum dated August 27 1930. Note the black-edged notepaper - her sister, Mary, had died in April of that year.

St Anne's school built in 1845 on land previously owned by Mr John Boon. The cost was £450 and the first headmaster and headmistress were Mr and Mrs George Holloway. About 1909 by means of a mortgage for £900 the school was enlarged to nearly double its original size. *'The repayment of the mortgage together with the necessary expenses for the upkeep of the school premises has been a heavy burden but the last installment was paid in 1941. From now on the school premises can be better cared for.'* (Rev T Lawton 1944)

St Anne's School 1900. Back: 1st left ?Hargreaves.

St Anne's School c 1906 with teacher Kate Proctor (Lovatt) on the left.
Back: 4th Charlotte Sheldon 2nd row: 5th left Martha Hargreaves

St Anne's School 1898 with William Jones, Headmaster. 3rd row: 4th Annie Hargreaves.
4th row: 4th Lydia Shirley (Pickford) who was later a teacher at the school. 5th row: 1st Thomas Hodkinson, 3rd Jack Snape.

ABOVE: St Anne's C of E School School Group with Mr William Jones (headmaster) c1912. Front entrance on School Bank before it was altered in 1910 when the school was extended. Mr Jones was the 7th Head in 10 years but remained for 40 years. He died in Cheshire in 1935 age 82. Lottie Grindy (Hayes) is here.

LEFT: Infant School c 1912. William Scarlett back row, third from left.

BELOW: St Anne's School 1920.

St Anne's School Sports Day 1932 on School Bank. Lily Jervis (Dawson) on the left and Belle Hodkinson (Lovatt). Belle's card said *'Consider the lilies of the field and how they grow'*. The first school sports day was held on 24 July 1920. It was organized by the new headmaster, Mr Walter Jones. After the judging of the fancy dress there was a procession round the village led by the brass band, finishing at Durber's field (Singlet House). A silver medal was awarded to the child with the most points, the first recipient being Ethel Sherratt. Points were awarded for fancy dress and sports winners and the one with the most points was school champion for the year.

A view of St Anne's School from Chapel Lane showing the school garden in the centre. The land for the garden was fenced in 1904 and set out in three sections. There was an orchard, a section for an evening class for boys who had left school and a section for boys in school. There was a tool shed and a cold frame. An inspector's report of 1930 praised the garden which by then had a large greenhouse and rock and water gardens.

School garden St Anne's School c1931
Back: Arthur Sherratt, Fred Dawson, Enoch Simcock
4th row: Fred Berrisford, - -, Jack Nixon
3rd row: George Snape, Joe Cumberlidge, ?, Bill Lowe, Fred Tomkinson
2nd row: Dennis Morris, Frank Frost, Levi Fox
Front: Norman Grindy, Arthur Berrisford, Harry Frost, Jack Sheldon, ? Alcock.

St Anne's School 1914. Esther Heath is on the front row, 2nd right.

St Anne's School 1920. Gladys Tomkinson's (Hammond) class

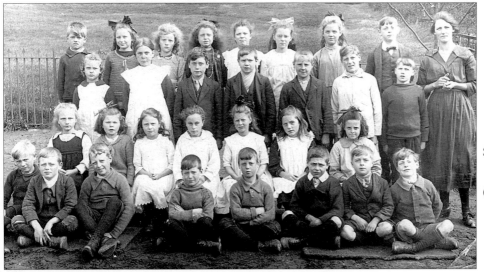

St Anne's School c 1922. Miss Honor Dawson (Benton) teacher. Gladys's class again.

1921 School group with headmaster, Mr Walter Jones.
Back: 9th Nellie Hargreaves
Third Row: 1st Phyllis Davenport, 3rd Miriam Hargreaves
Second Row: 3rd Colin Simcock, 5th Joe Berrisford
Front: 2nd Jack Sheldon, 9th Bill Hodkinson.

Bob Cumberlidge and his
sister Annie outside the
school c 1920.
Bob died in 1985,
Annie in 2007.

1944. New Lane before any
building was done.
The cutting also shows the
school bell in position.
Who are the boys?
The newspaper cutting said:
'The village school at Brown
Edge, built from the stone
which is characteristic of this
high moorland ridge.

The Old Infant School in Church Road

Records say that on 6th November 1851 Mr Hugh Henshall Williamson, from Greenway Bank bought land from Charles Hale, on which to build a parsonage and a new infant school, with headmistress's cottage attached. The new school was situated near to the parsonage, which was completed in 1853. Previously the infant school had been at Little Stonehouse Farm with Miss Beech as schoolmistress. A church magazine of 1871 lists Miss Large as mistress and in trade directories for 1876 and 1900 the mistress is Miss Alcock. When the new council infant school was built in 1910 the old infant school was converted into 2 cottages. Belle Hodkinson moved there with her family in 1931. It was then called West View, 56, Lane Ends. The house was bought from Jonathan Dawson and Fred Turner lived next door in the other cottage. Belle remembers that the pantry door in the kitchen was the original classroom door. Belle left in 1954 when she married Harry Lovatt and her mother stayed there until 1969. Pat Carter has lived there since 1974.

Belle Hodkinson. The official Sentinel photo when she was Hospital Queen in 1936. Belle lived in the old infants' school until she married Harry Lovatt in 1954. Her parents were Alice and Thomas Hodkinson.

ABOVE:
A cousin, Beryl Selby, outside West View when the old school still had mullion windows c 1958.

Alice Hodkinson (Belle's mother) outside the old infants' school in Church Road 1940s. Alice's maiden name was Hargreaves, her parents were Charlotte and Arthur.

Belle's aunt, Annie Hargreaves. She was Alice's eldest sister and lived with them as she never married.

Belle Hodkinson with her three brothers in 1932.
L-R: Belle aged 8, Arthur 18, Frank 15 and Sam 21.
Belle still lives in Brown Edge. Frank now lives in Manchester.

Phyllis Davenport with May Berrisford in the 1940s. Miss Davenport taught at St Anne's from the 1920s until the early 1950s.

St Anne's School c 1951
Back: Rodney Davies, Bernard Crossley,
Russell Turner, Roy Lowe, Clive Taylor.
Front: Rosalind Rowley, Audrey Harrison,
Glennis Mitchell, Sheila Condliffe,
Kathleen Cunliffe.

Mr Brown's class c 1957. Back: ?, John Worthy, Robert Bourne, Peter Wiggins, Peter Dawson, Robert Willis, Geoffrey Simcock, Roy Lovell, Clive Simcock, Ian Harrison, John Proctor.
Middle: Kathleen Grimes, Jennifer Foster, Margaret Heath, Jean Middleton, Diane Cooper, Edna Hughes, Bernard Brown, Marie Pepper, ?, Susan Bailey, ?, Barbara Holdcroft.
Front: Michael Kirkham, Neil Bolton, Peter Charlesworth, Kerry Tanner, Roy Sheldon, Sheila Slater, ?, Clive Fielding, Zigmund Tylman, Mario Zameriski.

Coronation Sports Day, Singlet House fields. Graham Mitchell about to win the boys' race with John Fenton just behind.

St Anne's c1954. ?, Margaret Browne, Margaret Hancock, Carol Cooper, Pauline Snape, Judith Hewitt, Irene Mountford

St Anne's Junior School mid 1950s Class 3. Back: ?, ?, ?, Howard Ashman, George Clowes, ?, ? ,? ,? , Alan Beardmore, Peter Worthy, ?, Dave Davenport, Keith Tanner, David Sheldon, Keith Smith.
Middle: Judith Hewitt, Margaret Hancock, Margaret Bailey, Sandra Black, Margaret Bourne, Bernard Brown, Gwenyth Hammond, Joan Rowland, Carol Cooper, Irene Mountford, Pauline Snape.
Front: Danny Holdcroft, ?, Sylvia Hollins, Marjorie Johnson, ?, Rona Penn, Wendy Protherow, Mary Jameson, Marion Jameson, ?, Philip Gratton.

St Anne's School nativity cast c 1960 L-R: Arthur Sheldon, Trevor Johnson, ?, Iris Lancaster, Philip Durber, Margaret Fox, Robert Chadwick, John Pointon, ?, Peter Protheroe, ?.

Valley Head Infants School Easter Bonnet Parade 1979. Back: ?, Mark Mellor, Wendy Lovatt, Wendy Carter, Rebecca Berrisford, ?, ?, Amanda Machin, Russell Johnson, ?, ?.
Middle: Justin Pomelli, Ashley Miller, Amanda Turner, Kelvin ?, Lee Hodgkinson, ?, Karen Hudson, Zoe Johnson, Paul Hornby, Robert Turner, Claire Turner, Kerry Vernon, Adam Wilson. Front: ?, Toni Miller, Sam Fox, Scott Brooks, ?, ?, Ben Fallows, ?, Jill Cumberlidge, ?, ?, ?, ?.

Valley Head Infants' School pantomime (Aladdin) c 1979. Some members of the cast: Justin Pomelli, Amanda Turner, Joanne Clewes, Paul Williams, Wendy Carter, Zoe Johnson, Toni Miller, Samantha Underwood, Jill Cumberlidge.

Tree Planting at St Anne's outside the Headmaster's house, March 1974.
Back: Melanie Huxley, Stephen Tinsley, Paul ?, Mark Beckett, Julie Hargreaves, Louise Harvey, Mr Ellis (headmaster), Janet Nicholls, Mr D C Wright (County Planning Officer).
Front: Paul Hargreaves, ? Jones, Stephen Frost, Jane Fox, Jane Durber, Andrea Webb, Herbert Bourne with grand-daughter Sheridan Ball.

BELOW:
Robin Hood at St Anne's School, January 1962.

ROBIN HOOD

A Pantomime by J. H. Turner

BROWN EDGE JUNIOR SCHOOL

Thursday and Friday, January 4th and 5th, 1962.   7-15 p.m.

Chairman :
Thursday : Mrs. A. WHISTON (Brown Edge)
Friday : NURSE R. A. CARTLIDGE (Brown Edge)

ADMISSION BY PROGRAMME
2s. 6d.
including refreshments. Children Half Price

Proceeds for St. Anne's Church Queen's Effort

Robin Hood

Characters in order of appearance		ACT 1
DERWENT	Alan Simcock	**Robin Hood's Camp in Sherwood Forest**
LITTLE JOHN	Ian Harrison	
WILL SCARLET	Paul Harvey	*INTERVAL*
FRIAR TUCK	Noel Carroll	
ROBIN HOOD	Clive Turner	**ACT 2**
NOSIE ROSIE (a cook)	Sheila Gladwyn	
LADY NYLON (the Sheriff's sister)	Lynn Foster	**A Room in Nottingham Castle**
SIR RICHARD OF THE LEA	Robert Mountford	
RODNEY (his Squire)	Jean Bartlam	
MAID MARION	Julia Tyler	Outlaws : Iris Lancaster, Anne Egan, Irene Foster, Kay Bartlam, Lynda Goodwin
WIMPEY PIMPEY (Court Jesters)	Anne Garsky Valerie Hewitt	Drums and Effects : David Willis, Paul Carroll
CAPTAIN HORSECOLLAR (of the Sheriff's Guards)	Veronica Snape	Produced for the Queen's Effort by IRENE TURNER
SHERIFF OF NOTTINGHAM	Graham Abbott	Assistant to Producer : Merle Harvey

Endon Secondary School George
and the Dragon c 1949
Back: Mr Lofthouse,
? Shufflebotham, Miss Thompson
Front: Meda Adams, ?, Florence
Adams, Merle Tyler, Lorna Durber,
Eddie Simcock, Barbara Morton,
Phil Rogers, John Landon.

RIGHT:
Endon Secondary School c 1950
Front: Mrs Hancock, ?, ?, Laura
Moss, ?, Mr Lofthouse
2nd: John Sherratt, Betty Sumner, ?.
3rd row: ?, ?.
Back: ?, Nora Proctor, ?.

BELOW: Endon Secondary
School staff early 1960s.
Back: ?, Mr Ballham, Mr
Heywood, ?, ?, ?, ?.
Middle: Mr Benton, Mr Parry, Mr
Smith, ?, ?, ?, Mr Dolan.
Front: ?, Mrs Edge, Mrs
Hancock, Mrs Benton, Mr
Hawley, Mr Eardley, Miss Leese,
?, Miss Tomkinson.

Endon School c 1947
Front: 3rd John Harvey, 6th Michael Burgess, 7th Derek ?, 8th Graham Jervis
2nd row: 7th Jean Knight, 8th Pam Plant, 9th Doris Moss
3rd row: 3rd Rosemary Proctor. Back: 8th Joe Adams, 9th Arthur Brown.

Endon Secondary School mid 1950s.
Standing L-R: Clive Foster, John Foster, Charles Simcock, Margaret Mayer, Pauline Sheldon, Jean Convery,
Jim Hudson, Nellie Horton, Brian Mountford, Shirley Brassey, Sylvia Brown, Terry Pointon,
David Berrisford, Raymond Holdcroft, Malcolm Gratton.
Seated: Maureen Bott, Elaine Fradley, June Willott, Ann Beech, Deanna Durber, Kathleen Price, Joyce Dawson.

Endon Secondary School 1954, Trent House with Headmaster Mr S Edwards. Chris Tatton at the back.
Some of the names are: Glennis Goodwin, Duncan Stewart, Maureen Haines, Valda Scarlett, Michael Heath,
Gillian Mountford, John Bourne, Evelyn Lowe, Wendy Hancock, Ivor Jones, Raymond Holdcroft, Beryl Firkins,
Maureen Davies, H Brindley, Christine Berrisford, Pat Evans, Doreen Unwin, Maureen Bott, June Willott.

Endon School Prizegiving 1969.
Standing: ? Edwards, Geoff Perkins, ?, Eric Elliott, Jim Clewes, ?, Ros Durber, Herbert Bourne, Harold Mear, ?.
Sitting: ?, ?, ? Robson, Betty Mosedale, W Hawley (Headmaster).

'Eminent old boy opens Endon School fair'
Nov 1976. Harry Hammond,
Philip Durber, David Steele, Alf Steele,
Gladys Hammond.
*'England cricketer, David Steele, was
besieged by autograph hunters when he
went back to his old school, Endon High, to
open an Autumn Fair. The fair was a
notable success, raising £700 for school
funds thanks to a turnout of over 600
parents and friends'.* (Leek Post and Times)

BELOW: Endon School 1940s.
Includes Doris Moss, Beryl Hulland,
Brenda Knight, Vera Baddeley.

Endon School 1967. Back: Ivan Kindrat, David Johnson, Keith Hubble, ?, Ian Watts,
David Williams, Terry Hall, Ronnie Jenkins, Alan Cole, Tony Kent, Peter Berrisford, Mervin Flute.
Middle: Maureen Cleghorne, Andrew Brassington, Martin Simcock, Tony Evans.
Front: Linda Reeves, Angela Fitzgerald, Yvonne Shelley, Ada Clewes, Elizabeth Wardle, Janet Jones, Mr Clarke,
Rosamond Durber, Freda Unwin, Wendy Murphy, Valerie Hughes, Janet Lucking.

Before the church was built there were two huge rocks - one of which was levelled for the building of four houses, the other to make one of the grandest of sites on which to build the Church. It is a veritable *'house built upon a rock'*. Rev TD Lawton 1944. The Nave was completed in 1844 and consecration took place on 29 May 1844 with five to six hundred people present. To mark completion of the Nave a silver medal was struck and one was presented to every male parishioner of 70 years or over. The spire was completed in 1854 and the vicarage was completed in 1853.

Mary Durber as Queen c 1928 probably Hill Top Chapel.

RIGHT: James William Basnett. He was taken ill while ringing in the New Year of 1928 at the church. He was carried to his home, Bleak House, on a door and died a few hours later.

LEFT: Jean Horne as Hospital Queen 1937 outside her home, Smithy Cottage in Sandy Lane. Jean was presented with a bible by Mr Leigh with the inscription: *Presented to Miss Jean Horne by Mr W Leigh on the occasion of her coronation at Brown Edge Hospital Carnival as Coronation Queen. July 24 1937.*

A function at St Luke's Mission, Hill Top early 1930s.
Back: Bill Lowe, Charlie Davenport, ?, Bill Biddulph, ?, May Durber, Elsie Durber, Edith Harvey, Edith Lomas, Dorothy Lowe, Stanley Davenport
Front: ? , Frances Biddulph, Doris Lomas, Ivy Berrisford, Harold Harvey with son Harold, Nora Dawson, Gertie Lowe, Vera Lomas

The first Church and also Centenary Queen, Janet Proctor, with her retinue outside her home, Sunny Bank in High Lane, 1944

St Anne's Church Queen, Wendy Scragg. 1952
Back: Alan Beardmore, Jennifer Proctor, Irene Schofield, Audrey Durber, Wendy, Lila Goodwin, Beryl Selby, ? Hargreaves.
Front: Pamela Cumberlidge, May Hargreaves and Ann Hurst.

St. Anne's Church
Brown Edge.
Renovation Fund.

GARDEN PARTY
at
Poole Fields, Brown Edge.
Saturday, July 22nd 1944

The programme for the first church queen and garden party.

Procession Marshall:-
Mr G. Bond.

Assemble at
'Sunny Side', High Lane
at 2.15 pm.
Move off 2.30 pm

Proceed to Church
via Sytch

Service in Church 3 pm.

Proceed to Poole Fields.
via St. Anne's Vale.

Centenary Queen
Janet Proctor.

Assembly — 4 pm
Queen's Parade
Chairman's Address
(Mr H Moreton)
Crowning Ceremony and
Opening: Mr J Hebblethwaite
Presentation to Opener
by Betty Jolly
Presentation to Chairman
by Katherine Holdcroft
Tableau by Sunday School Scholars
Acrobatic Display. Marion Latham
Dancing by Brindley Ford Scholars
Play and Puppet Show by
Norton C. of E. Scholars
Votes of Thanks
    Mr H. Proctor
    Mr G. Hall

Numbers 7, 8 and 9 will be
repeated after Tea

The Victory Parade on School Bank 1946

Church Queen 1946, Doris Moss, at Rock Cottage. Behind Doris is June and Joy Willott. Mavis Ford is at the back.

British Legion Queen, Joyce Dawson c 1947. Some members of the retinue are : Deirdre Worthy, Alan Hancock, Kenneth Snape, ? Beff, ? Paddock, Betty Condliffe.

Joyce Lowe in Mavis Ford's retinue.

Mavis Ford, Church Queen 1947, and retinue at Rock Cottage.

RIGHT: Sandy Lane Chapel Fete.
Gladys Mountford and Iris Clarke.

Carnival at Pool Fields 1947 Back: Gladys Hammond, Rev FS Ramsden, Staffs Coal Queen, Doris Moss, Mavis Ford, Joan Proctor, ?, Harry Proctor. Graham Mitchell sitting in front of Doris. Others include Beryl Selby, June Willott, Ann Morris, John Foster, ? Nixon, Frank Selby, Malcolm Mitchell, Lila Hollins, Pauline Tomkinson, Margaret Wright, John Fenton.

Sandy Lane Chapel Outing c 1950. The Chapel seen on the right was sold in 1980 and later demolished. Some of the travellers are: Albert and Gladys Mountford, Irene Mountford, Mr and Mrs Adderley, Joy Tatton, Clara Weaver.

BELOW:
Jean and Denis Holdcroft with their children Stuart & Gary. Sandy Lane chapel in background

Albert Mountford in Sandy Lane with Sheila Condliffe lcft and daughter, Irene. Mr Mountford was Sunday School Superintendent at Sandy Lane Chapel. He was born at Norton Green and was a butcher, later a mechanic and worked as a garage foreman at Whitfield Colliery.
He married Gladys Slack and they had two children - Brian and Irene. He died 2001 aged 89.

All aboard at Sandy Lane Chapel Fete on Weaver's Field, St Anne's Vale c 1950.
Back: Albert Mountford, Betty Condliffe, Maureen Baddeley, Gladys Mountford, Thelma Bettney, Dorothy Weaver, Joy Weaver, Flo Simcock, child - Irene Mountford.
Front: Louis Adams, John Bourne, ?, Russell Turner, Graham Docksey, ?, Ray Adams, Neville Condliffe, Brian Mountford, Michael Turner.

Rev Walter Attoe with his wife, Peggy and children Rosemary and David.
Rev Attoe was the vicar at St Annes from 1950-1956.

Rev Attoe - getting into the part - and Mrs Attoe.

LEFT: These gorgeous girls are actually Dick Turner, Bill Bourne and Tom Mitchell.

BELOW:
A mock wedding 1950s. An unusual idea for raising money for the church. A 'bride and groom' in full wedding regalia sit down to a meal with their 'guests'. The ladies arrive dressed as men and the men as women. Each couple bring a wedding present to be raffled off. The 'bride and groom' are Norah Baddeley and Arthur Garner. All were members of the Church drama group. Nora borrowed the dress from a friend and the cake was created by Leah Crossley. L-R: ?, Linden Evans, Bob Cumberlidge, Brian Proctor, Norah Baddeley, Arthur Garner, Mary Harvey, Dick Turner, Jesse Clements, ?, Tom Mitchell.

A mock wedding group - who are these people?

Sandy Lane Chapel Queen Sandra Beff (Hancox)1955.

Church Nativity c 1953
Back: Rosemary Proctor as the angel
Middle: Brian Proctor, Bob Cumberlidge, Alice Cumberlidge, Gwen Turnock, ?, Tom Mitchell, Annie Mitchell, Joy Willott, John Fenton Senr, Rev Attoe, Bill Bourne
Front: John Holdcroft, ? Paddock?, John Fenton, John Foster, David Holdcroft

Maypole dancers on their way to the fete in the 1940s. Some of the dancers are Sheila Hammond, Valerie Bettany, Cath Meredith, Hazel Chadwick, Margaret Wright, Florence Adams, Merle Tyler, June Bourne, Glenys Hancock and Hilary Walker.

The church weathercock was re-gilded in 1946 with other restoration work. Donald Heath on right worked for Blackburn and Starling who did some of the work.

July 25 1946 the six bells were transported to Taylor's Bell Foundry Loughborough to be turned. On return they were re-hung on a new steel frame and re-dedicated 19 January 1947. A tea was provided in the school. The little boy is Alan Pointon, son of Sam Pointon. Alan remembers some of the stonework had to be removed to get the bells out of the door. The replacement stone can still be seen.

Drama Group - *Storm in a Big Cup*.
Back: Jack Nixon, Bill Bourne, Dick Turner, George Bond, Ted Wright, Bob Cumberlidge
Front: Dolly Proctor, Hilda Proctor, Madge Bond, Mrs Mountford, Leah Crossley, Mrs Wright, Joan Simmons, Elsie Bourne

St Anne's Church Drama Group, 1950s - Mrs Wiggs of the Cabbage Patch.
L-R: Tom Mitchell, Teddy Wright, ?, Madge Bond, Hilda Proctor, Mrs Frank Proctor, Leah Crossley

St Anne's Church Queen, Gwenyth Hammond, outside the Vicarage 1956
L-R: Albert Nixon (People's Warden), Gladys Hammond, Rev W Attoe, Mrs H Taylor, Gwenyth, Miss Barrett, Mrs Attoe, Major Stephen Johnson (opener of the fete), George Hall (vicar's warden)

1954 St Anne's Church Queen, Elizabeth Charles in the garden of Rock Cottage.
L-R: Pauline Turner, Glennis Mitchell, John Simmons, John Worthy, June Hancock, Elaine Lowe, Rosemary Attoe, Elizabeth, ? Bourne, ? Morris.

Sandy Lane Chapel ladies 1951.
Back: Iris Clarke, Beryl Matijevic, Doris Condliffe, Minnie Heath, Hannah Dale, Lillian Heath (Bourne)Cissie Hawley, Cary Lovatt.
Middle: Gladys Weaver, Sarah Ann Goodwin, Ethel Foster, Mrs Worthy.
Front: Clara Weaver, Mrs Pointon, Gladys Mountford, Mrs Sant, Clara Dutton, Ellen Willott, Freda Berrisford, ?.

'Peddlar's Fayre' in St Anne's School 1956. Raising money for a new heating installation - £600 being required. The queen's retinue moved among the patrons 'pedalling their wares'. Bill Hollins launched a mile of pennies scheme for the fund. Left: Ann Morris, Bill Hollins, Gladys Hammond, Mrs E Garrett (opener), ?, Elizabeth Charles, Mrs Attoe, Ann Hurst, George Hall, J H Turner, Rev W T D Attoe. Front: Susan Bailey, Judith Berrisford, Carol Cooper, Gwenyth Hammond. Also pictured Joyce Scarlett and Elsie Morris.

St Anne's Church Festival when the queen was Leila Hollins 1951
Standing: Gladys Hammond, Alderman W Hancock, Horace Proctor, Ethel Foster.
Seated: Mrs Hancock (opener), Rev W T D Attoe, Alderman Mrs Barker (who crowned the queen). The programme for this event says *'Teas - running buffet - suppers - floodlight dancing in the Vicarage grounds - firework display... and so to bed'.*

Presentations at school to Rev WD Attoe & Mrs Attoe 1956
Standing: ?, Rev WD Attoe, George Hall, Albert Nixon
Seated: ?, Alderman William Hancock, Mrs Attoe, Mrs Hancock.
Rev Attoe returned to Brown Edge to open the carnival and fete in 1970 when he was vicar of St John's Church, Wolverhampton.

Church of England Children's Society (formerly waifs and strays) was founded in 1881. Each year there was a Founder's Day Festival in the Royal Albert Hall and for a number of years a village group went to London to present purses to the Society - in 1957 a party of nine went.

Back: Mrs Heath, Rosemary Proctor, Mrs Hammond, Rev RG Lansdale

Front: Hazel Heath, Mrs Black, Sandra Black, Gwenyth Hammond, Ethel Forster.

Gladys Hammond (nee Tomkinson)

Gladys was born in 1910 in a cottage on Fiddler's Bank, the 7th of 11 children of Jonathan and Sarah Ann Tomkinson. She went to Brown Edge School and then worked in the mills in Leek. She married Harry Hammond, a weaver. Gladys was always involved with St Anne's Church, a member of the Choir and Mother's Union. She often went to London for the presentation of purses and was involved in the annual Church Fete - she trained a generation of children when to bow or curtsey. He was a member of the parish council and Leek RDC - he was Chairman in 1966/67. Harry was the village undertaker with his friend Billy Booth from Biddulph Moor. Harry died in 1979. Gladys was a founder member of the Over 60's and served as their treasurer until she was nearly 90. She loved singing and sang solo in Lichfield Cathedral on several occasions. She was part of a group from the Over 60's who toured the area entertaining other pensioner groups. She died in October 2004 aged 94.

Gwenyth Hammond and Elizabeth Charles present the purses to the Queen Mother, 1954.

Visitors to the Albert Hall again take time off in Trafalgar Square. L-R: Mary Holdcroft, Lottie Hayes, Gladys Hammond, Hilda Berrisford, ?, Nellie Berrisford, Mrs Jim Proctor. Children are left, Dianne Hodgkinson and Deirdre Worthy.

Harvest at the Roebuck October 1958
Back: Betty Mitcheson, Nellie Worthy, Ethel Farrington, Jack Farrington.
Middle: George Hall, ? Dawson, Horace Hayes, Bill Redfern, Chris Hargreaves, ?, John Crossley, Denis Mosedale.
Front: George Chadwick, Rev RG Lansdale, Lottie Hayes, Bill Protheroe

1958 Susan Bailey, queen elect, leading the procession from the church to the school for the crowning ceremony.

1950. Procession down St Anne's Vale. Rock House in the background. Sandy Lane Chapel Queen, Margaret Bourne.

Sports Day 1967
Standing: Clive Turner, Margaret Heath, Enock Goodwin, Albert Mountford, Norman Lomax, Rev HW Jones, ?, Diane Cooper
Seated: Barbara Atkins, Sylvia Lomax, Arthur Pointon, Iris Clarke, Mr Clarke.

Susan Bailey with Rev RG Lansdale. The vestry table was donated by Gladys and Jack Bailey, Susan's parents, and is still in use.

LEFT: Sandy Lane Chapel Sports Day, Sept. 1967.
Fancy Dress Winners L-R: Andrew Atkins, Ian Clark, Jill Beckett.

A Day Out to New Brighton for members of Hill Top Chapel Youth Club.
Back: Clive Proctor, Chris Tatton, Ray Parr, Mike Nicholls, Dave Harvey, Tony Hodkinson
Front: Kathleen Cumberlidge, Ann Hughes, ?, Pat Worthy, Hazel Nicholls.

The carnival field behind Rose Cottage, Church Rd, 1956.

Harvest Supper in the school c1957
Standing: George Hall, Beattie Holdcroft, Doreen Knight, Margaret Clements, Jesse Jolley, Mrs Hall, ?, ?, Herbert
Bourne, Margaret Hargreaves, Yvonne Hargreaves, Mrs Clements
Seated: Flo Hancock, Bill Hancock, Dennis Pryce, Margaret Pryce, Roy Knight, Thomas Lowe.
Children: Gwen and Kerry Knight.

1953 The crowning of St Anne's Church queen, Dierdre Worthy, by Lady Sylvia Rose Chetwynd-Talbot, daughter of the Earl and Countess of Shrewsbury.
Back: Wendy Scragg, Dierdre, Lady Sylvia, Mrs A E Bennett, Alderman Bennett, Rev W T Attoe, Gladys Hammond, Alderman W Hancock, ?, Doreen Unwin
Front : ?, Susan Bailey, ?, ?, Ann Lowe, ?, Gwenyth Hammond, John Holdcroft.

RIGHT: A presentation to Mr George Hall, bellringer. Other ringers:
Standing: Alan Pointon, Bob Cumberlidge, Rev WT Attoe, Alf Cottrell, Billy Bourne, Bert Pointon, Sam Pointon. Seated: Bill Dean, Tom Taylor, George Hall, Frank Holdcroft, Dick Turner.
Front: John Hargreaves, John Fenton, Robert Bailey, Fred Snape.

BELOW:
May 1963, Evening Service, Children's Mission Week at St Anne's.
Back: Rev PJ Lafford, St Chad's Church, Leicester and Rev E Richards, Brown Edge.

Barbecue at Newfold Farm c 1970. This event was to raise money for the Church Lychgate Fund.
L-R: ?, Yvonne Hargreaves, ?, ?, Denis Mosedale, Sammy Slade, Harry Frost, Reg Twemlow, Marjorie Twemlow.

1973 St Anne's Grand Carnival Gymkhana held at Willfield Farm.
A bevy of beauties:
Back: Julie Snape, Diane Cooper, Jill Snape, Pamela Bartlam,
Middle: Diane Tatton, Lynn Tatton, Karen Lovatt, Louise Harvey
Front: Jane Durber, Cathy Durber, Julie Walker, Christine Johnson.

St Anne's Church Queen, Michelle Hargreaves 1977, Silver Jubilee.
Back: Yvonne Hargreaves, Mrs Wood, Sharon Bowler, ?, Ann Thickett, Rachel Watkins, Michelle.
Front: Paul Cumberlidge, Mary Lovatt, Angela Turner.
The queen was crowned by Mrs Brian Hilditch, a leading singer with Newcastle Operatic Society.
The international racing cyclist, Reg Harris, was a special guest.

Baby Show at St Anne's Fete August 17th 1968. Back: ?, ?, Nancy Bell with Robert, Julie Baker with Robert, Angela Mountford with Debbie, ?, ?. Front: ?, Marjorie Snape with Andrew, Joan Adams and Mark, Glenys Sargeant and Alison, Josie White and Tony. The winning baby was Tony White and he won some Cow and Gate baby food and a small Doulton ornament.

Carnival Army Patrol with Sylvia Hayes, Sheila Holt and Beryl Hulstone.

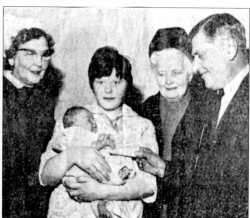

Robert Bell on the baby show photo was the first baby to be born at the old maternity unit at City General Hospital, on March 31st 1968.

St Anne's Church Queen, Sharon Turner, 1965. L-R: Fiona Huxley, Janet Scott, Pamela Bartlam, Andrew Scott, Sharon, Julia Baddeley, Janice Snape, Carol Mathews, Jill Pickstock.

1973 St Anne's Carnival best float was the cub scouts' Snow White and the Seven Dwarfs. Andrew Walker as Snow White, Mark Beckett as Bashful and John Hayes.

Michelle with Rev. A Moseley and visitors at the Autumn Fayre 1977

July 1994, 50th Anniversary of St Anne's Church Queen and 150th anniversary of the church.
Centre
Front: 1994 queen, Samantha Turner with Janet Downing (nee Proctor) the first queen in 1944.

The Church with the old pews down each side and chairs in the centre. A text over the Chancel Arch reads *'Surely the Lord is in this place'*. This must have been painted over. The stone tablets either side of the arch had the Ten Commandments on them.

Below:
The wedding of Joan Priestman and Clifford Orpe. The small bridesmaid is Pauline Tomkinson. The text over the Chancel Arch can be seen.

The Vicar, Churchwardens and Church Council of St. Anne's Church, Brown Edge,

invite

Brown Edge "Over 60" Club.

to the

Dedication of the New Seats

by

The Bishop of Stafford,

on Thursday, June 2nd, 1966,

St Anne's Church
The Dedication of the New Seats June 2 1966.

Fred Hulstone giving rides to children at St Anne's Church Fete 1976. The crowning and Fete was held in the playground of the Infant School because work was being done on extensions to St Anne's.

Jackie Snape as St Anne's Church Queen, 1968
Back: Gladys Hammond, Mavis Snape with Mandy
Front: Kevin Snape, Pamela Simcock, Janice Turner, Jackie, Gail Tatton, Julie Lear, Joanne Barlow, Duncan Barlow.

Sandy Lane Chapel 1957.
Back: Sandra Beff, Sheila Slater, Irene Mountford, Pam Cumberlidge.
Front: ?, ?, John Baker, ?, ?, Gordon Turner, Terry Slater.

Mary Ellen Grindy (nee Tomkinson) with her
children William (Bill) and
Charlotte (Lottie) c 1909.
They lived at Fairview, Bank End.

Bill and Lottie Grindy c 1912. Lottie married Horace Hayes and
kept the Roebuck. Bill bought a field in Sandy Lane, off George
Hargreaves in 1934 and built Thelma Avenue with 21 houses. He
named it after his daughter (now Thelma Steele).

Mr Powell lived in an old cottage in St Anne's Vale

Members of the Scragg family outside High Tor, Top
Chapel Lane. L-R: Fred, Clara Scragg (nee Jolley)
holding Geoffrey (father of Wendy and Hilary Scragg)
Hugh (father) with Henshall.
Clara was pictured haymaking with her sisters on the
back cover of *Brown Edge Memories*.
Clara and Hugh had 10 children.

The cottage in Broad Lane opposite Steinfields Farm L-R: Sam Hodkinson, John (Jack) Sheldon, Bill Hodkinson, Mary Alice Sheldon, Sam Sheldon, ?, Joe Holdcroft. Jack, Sam and Mary Alice were three of the children of Sam and Hannah Sheldon (nee Cumberlidge).

Pauline Sheldon (Higginbotham) was born at Steinfields Farm, Broad Lane, in 1942. Her dad, Sam Sheldon was born at the cottage opposite in 1913 and was at Steinfields Farm for 38 years. The farm was 14 acres.

ABOVE: Wedding of Sam Sheldon and Minnie Harvey (Pauline's mother and dad) April 1938.
Back: Jack Sheldon, Sam and Minnie, Luke Harvey.
Front: Edith Harvey, Mary Harvey.

LEFT: A family wedding at Mossley Church 1950.
Back: George Brown, Mrs Brown, Mary Davenport, Nora Davenport.
Front: Minnie Sheldon, Hannah Sheldon, Sam Sheldon (Pauline's granddad), Elsie Brown, Sam Sheldon (Dad)
Front: Colin Sheldon.

Jack Sheldon with his wife Annie (nee Ferns) and son
Desmond. Jack died in 1938 aged 28.

Grace Sheldon dated on the back of the photo Oct 18, 1907.
Grace was the daughter of Richard Sheldon, long-serving
licensee of The Lump of Coal. Richard married Jane Dawson
in 1860 and they had 11 children. Grace married Joseph
Cumberlidge and was the mother of Annie Shallcross.

Pauline's mum, Minnie Sheldon (Nee
Harvey) in 1937, aged 26.

Luke and Minnie Harvey with their daughter Edith in late
1920s. These are Pauline's grandparents who lived at
Bluestone Cottages.They moved to Boardman's Bank (where
the Lowes live). Luke Harvey's brother was Isaac who was
caretaker of St Luke's Mission, Hill Top.

John Chadwick 1936

John Chadwick: Chadwick's paper shop

I was born in 1934 and my parents were Charles and Violet Chadwick. Mother's maiden name was Dawson and she came from Smallthorne. I have two brothers, Robert and Malcolm. I lived in The Vale for a while then Dad bought a house in Mountford's Row for £200. The Chadwick family were always blacksmiths on the village - my grandfather, Ben and great grandfather, Joseph. There was a Smithy opposite the Roebuck up Piggy Lane and also one in Sandy Lane, at the bottom of Hough Hill.

In 1920 my grandfather Jim Chadwick opened a paper shop where he lived in Mountford's Row. I used to go with him to collect the papers from Stockton Brook, they came on the bonnet of a bus. Grandfather had a barrow and we used to wheel the papers up then deliver them. Later dad made him a trolley. I was the paper lad up St Anne's Vale when I was about nine and knew everybody. Near where the Tab was there used to live an old man named Powell. In the winter when it was snowing Mr Powell used to see me coming and he'd hang this bacon on the old hob, with bread underneath and all the dripping going on to it - a lovely bacon sandwich! Mrs Basnett at Bleak House used to make me lobby as well. I delivered morning and nights and still did it when I went to Endon School. Later Arnold Sant bought the paper round off granddad. He had a paper shop opposite Garner's shop, next to the Band Room.

The wedding of Charles Chadwick and Violet Dawson at Brown Edge Church 1934 (John's parents).

John's grandparents James and Hannah Chadwick outside their house at 3 Mountford's Row where they had the newsagents c 1942.
Hannah died in 1951 age 74 and James in 1952 age 79.

Grandfather Jim Chadwick.

Violet, left, and Elsie Chadwick c1919.

John's mum Violet Chadwick (nee Dawson) c 1919

Dawson's shoe shop Smallthorne c 1910. It was opposite where Sammy Lowe's chip shop is now. L-R: ?, Caleb Dawson (Violet's father), Margaret Dawson (Violet's mother), ?, Caleb made the shoes in the cellar and was the first locally to make shoes for the disabled.

The Davenport family behind their home, The Gables in St Annes Vale. Mum and Dad, (Annie and Harry) with Dave left and Stan right. Annie's maiden name was Gratton. The house was built by Harold Bourne and the family moved there in 1941. Harry's Grandma and Grandad Davenport used to live next door at The Beeches. Their daughter, Mary had The Gables built in 1930.

Dave and Stan's dad, William Henry Davenport (Harry), right with his brother Jack. Harry was born at Apple Tree Farm in 1909. He also had two sisters, Eileen and Eva. He went to St Anne's School then Leek High School. He worked at Radway Green during the war. The family moved to Brookdene in High Lane, next to Turner's garage which can be seen in the background.

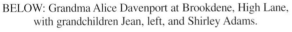

BELOW: Grandma Alice Davenport at Brookdene, High Lane, with grandchildren Jean, left, and Shirley Adams.

Annie Gratton, left, with Marie Sutton (Redfern)

Jack Davenport became a professional boxer. He used to do sparring sessions in the Band Room on a Sunday morning. During the war he was a tank driver in the eighth army with Mountbatten in Africa, then later in Germany. He died aged 71.

Joseph Arthur Simcock (Joe) outside his home on Fiddler's Bank. Joe was born at Job's Pool, the 5th of 13 children. Joe was a boxer. At the village fete in the late 1940s a boxing ring was set up and Joe sparred with Jack Davenport. In July 1947 he won the welterweight championship at the Victoria Hall, Hanley in the first round. He won £20 - £5 a punch. Joe is now 80 and lives in Middlewich, Cheshire.

Jane Willott with Duncan outside their house.

Betty Lowe: JANE WILLOTT

My mother was the eldest daughter of Elizabeth and Enoch Simcock of Lowe's Villa, Sandy Lane. She was caretaker of the Infant school for 30 years. Mum loved children and was never happier than when she was with them. She also helped people on the village at times of sickness or childbirth. She would always go if asked.

During the war Mum took in a 14 month old evacuee from Manchester named Duncan. He remained with us until he married at the age of 21. He married Pauline Durkin from Burslem and they emigrated to New Zealand in 1964.

They have two children, Melanie and Stephen, and now live in Palmerston, North Island. Stephen has three children, Benjamin, Tim and Gabriel.

Rachel Knight lived in 'Granny's Cottage' in Sytch Road and was Ernest Beff's mum. Rachel married John Alfred Beff from Buglawton and had five children - Ernest, Elsie, Annie (died at 19), William and Hannah. Rachel and John lived at Bluestone then moved to High Lane.

Rachel's brother, George Knight in 1955. George never married. He was the local 'knocker up', with the nickname of 'Quirl' and lived in High Lane next door to Helen Holdcroft's shop.

Agnes Fox's wedding to Joe Thompson. They lived at Star Farm.
L-R: Arthur Brassington, Joe, Agnes, Levi Fox.

The Fox family.
L-R: George, Florrie,
Joe, Levi, Vera seated.

Joseph Gratton served in the First World War. He bought Poolfields Farm in 1947. His wife was Mary Ann.

A family group. Mary Ann and Joseph Gratton standing. Seated are Jack and Maggie Jervis.

VERA WILLIS

Vera Willis (nee Gratton) was born in 1923 in Heath's Row and her parents were Joseph and Mary Ann Gratton (nee Jervis). Mary Ann died following a tragic accident when Vera was about 10. Her father later remarried and his wife was Lizzie Johnson, whose father kept a shop next to the Lump of Coal pub. Vera went to Brown Edge School and then worked in the mills at Leek. During the War she worked at British Aluminium. She later went to live with her grandparents, George and Lizzie Jervis, at Rose Cottage, Church Road. She married Albert Willis in 1944. They lived in the same house on School Bank all their married life and had two sons, Robert and David. Vera was the caretaker at the Tab for many years. She died in July 2009 age 85.

With local children at Lagos 1942.

ALBERT WILLIS

Albert was born at Brindley Ford in 1922. He first worked on a Pot Bank then became a miner, working at Chatterley Whitfield and Victoria collieries. His brother, Vincent, was the father of Mary Ellis. Albert served in the navy in World War II as a Stoker First Class. When he first applied for service at the age of 17 he was turned down, as mining was a reserved occupation. He applied the following year, said he was a pottery worker and was accepted.

Albert served on various convoy ships - *Tamarisk, Despatch, Durban* and *True Love* and was based in Sierra Leone. He remembers that in November 1945 his ship was in the Mediterranean on mine sweeping duties, when they learned of the Japanese surrender and 'spliced the main brace' (a double tot of rum). Albert was awarded five medals.

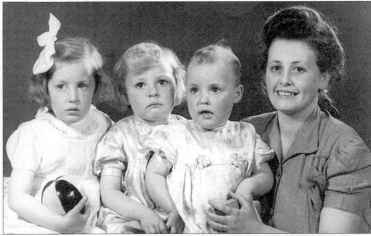

Mary Ann with three of her children: Joyce, Marjorie and Ann c1943. The family left Pool House in 1946.

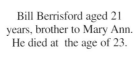

Bill Berrisford aged 21 years, brother to Mary Ann. He died at the age of 23.

Mary Ann Berrisford was born at Pool House, Job's Pool, to Lottie and James Berrisford. She was a nurse at Bucknall Hospital until she married Arnold Lowe.

The Lowe Family. Back: Marjorie, Ann, Joyce Front: Gillian, Paul, Mary Ann, Arnold holding Peter, Janet.

Mary Ann's Grandma Charlotte (Lottie) Berrisford (nee Sheldon) who also lived at Pool House.

James and Charlotte (Lottie) Berrisford with some of their children in early 1930s.
L-R: Harry, Charlotte, Lottie, Mary Ann and James.

A family portrait L-R: Joe, Zipporah and Fred Berrisford.   Mary Ann's uncle, Joseph Sheldon, known as 'Stumpy'.

Great Grandmother Jane Sheldon (nee Mottram). She was born in 1867. It is said she often rode bareback round the village

1928 May Brough aged 16. She married Joe Berrisford.

Brother Joe, aged 18.

May's parents, Jim and Charlotte Brough (nee Simcock)

Mary Scarlett age 21 in 1937.

George Scarlett in his garden in Sandy Lane with four of his children: L-R: Lottie, Evie, Hannah and Jim.

The Scarlett children: Jim, Hannah, Evie, Lottie and Bill c 1911.

Sam Scarlett who emigrated to Alberta, Canada in 1903.

Three likely lads. L-R: George Scarlett jr,
Stanley Scarlett, Jack Davenport

Harry Pointon with his wife, Sarah Anne with Hannah
Scarlett holding Lewis Pointon. The Pointons kept the shop
opposite the Band Room in the 1930s & 40s.

Mary Ann Basnett c 1896, the eldest daughter
of James W Basnett who built Bleak House.
She married George Scarlett.

Mary Scarlett
age 15.

Doris Moss standing with sister, Laura c 1940

Frank Moss with Laura outside their home, Willow Cottage, in Sandy Lane c 1954. The spaniel's name is Ginger.

Beatrice Moss (nee Lowe) from Hill Top.

Laura Moss with her children: Jennifer, Laura and Doris c 1946.

Doris Moss and Ron Stanway pose beside their Austin car.

Laura and Frank Moss at Hill Top c 1936.

Winnie Durber standing with Margaret Downes taken on Singlet Farm land (now Brownhills Road) c1930. Back Lane can be seen in the background.

Thomas Baddeley left, and brother Richard c1906.

RIGHT:
Hilda Hargreaves 1930s.

William and Hannah Durber of Ladymoor Gate Farm with their children. They later moved to Singlet House Farm.
Front: May, William with Winnie, Hannah with Harry, Dorothy. Back: William, Elizabeth, Arthur, Ethel, Dan, Jack. c 1903

John Harvey, grandsons Bill and Harvey Durber 1916.

Ann and Lizzie Durber c 1930.

Hannah Basnett c 1907. She was the
daughter of James W Basnett
and married Albert Edward Green.

Tom and Annie Mitchell (nee Bourne) with children Graham and Glennis.
Taken at Top Heath's Row in the late 1940s.
Annie was sister to Gladys Bailey.

William Durber and his daughter, Ethel, with Harry Durber standing. At Singlet House Farm.

THE TOMKINSON FAMILY

Jonathan Tomkinson married Sarah Ann Boon in 1895, at Leek Registry Office and they lived in Heath's Row in Church Road. Jonathan was the son of Joseph and Sarah Ann Tomkinson (nee Dawson). His grandparents, James Tomkinson and Hannah Hancock, were married at St Anne's Church in 1853. Jonathan was a miner/horse driver at Whitfield Colliery. Jonathan and Sarah Ann had eleven children. The eldest, Arthur, died of TB in 1928 aged 30. Two died in infancy. Of the remaining eight three married and moved to Leek - Lizzie,

Alice and Fred. The other five married and stayed in Brown Edge. Elsie married Sam Ellis and lived in Mountford's Row. Rose married Leonard Mitchell and lived next door to Gladys (who married Harry Hammond) in Quarry Lane off Church Road. May married John Fenton and lived in Heath's Row. Bill also lived in Heath's Row with his wife Vera. Bill is remembered as a cheerful conductor on Turner's buses. He was also a pigeon fancier with prize-winning birds.

Gladys Tomkinson c 1928.

Some of the Tomkinson Family. Gladys is front left.

Gladys on the right with her sister May.

Gladys's parents, Jonathan and Sarah Ann Tomkinson (nee Boon).

In 1902 a football team was organized by the Rev Sturdee and Mr Lance Jones (son of headmaster William Jones), One of the conditions of being a member of the team was to attend at least one service at St Anne's Church each week. This group is pictured outside the old Infants School in Church Road. They played in the field opposite.

Standing 1st left,
 James Herbert Pointon.

Seated: Sammy Turner,
Pel Turner, ?, ?, ?.

An early ladies' cricket team
c 1910.

Sandy Lane Football team
c 1919.
Back: 1st right Jim Snape
2nd right James Chadwick.

Members of the Gun Club c
1920s.
Standing: 2nd Bill Bowyer,
3rd James Chadwick, 7th
Tom Johnson. Seated 3rd
Dr Glass.

RIGHT: Time off at Knypersley
Pool 1930s.
Seated on bridge:
Ted Hodkinson, Joe Holdcroft, Bill
Hodkinson, Joe Hollins, Joe
Hodkinson.

BELOW:
A day out on George Mayer's bus
in the 1920s. Back: Sam Sheldon,
?, George Mayer, ?, ?, Alice
Mayer, Violet Higgins, ?, Nora
Davenport, ?, ?.
Front: ?, ?, Mary Davenport, ?,
Harriet Simcock, Hannah Sheldon,
?, Evie Scarlett (Barber), ?.

Above:
Bright Young Things late 1920s. Horace Espley, Reg Barber, Lottie Scarlett, Evie Scarlett, ?, ?, ?, We think the vehicle is an Austin 10.

Time out for a picnic. c 1940. Nellie Chadwick, Elsie Dono (nee Chadwick) and Arthur Dono.

Below:
Day out on Turner's bus. Driver Gordon Turner.

Brown Edge Football Team c 1916. Tom Baddeley 2nd from right and Tom Berrisford 1st left, front.

A day of leisure mid 1930s. Violet Higgins, Harriet Lowe, Ethel Dawson, Kate Lowe, Evelyn Harvey and Hannah Scragg.

Below:
Three unknown characters outside the front entrance of the Roebuck pub (now Keith's Workshop).

Below right: Marshes Hill late 1930s. Bill Biddulph at the back. Front: Jim Simcock, Reg Dawson, Fred Berrisford, Ernest Sherratt.

Joseph Scarlett who lived in Sandy Lane.
He was married to Hannah Clews and they had eight children.

Joe Horne of Sandy Lane. Joe and his
wife, Alice, lived for many years at
Smithy Cottage opposite the chip shop.

Saturday night at the Band Room 1950s.
Sitting on the stage Pat Price, Doris Moss, Doreen Hocknell, Kath Joyce.

Dave Scarlett and Alan Holdcroft 1959.

A trip to Blackpool c 1953: Cliff Johnson, Keith Eardley, John Chadwick,
Geoffrey Burgess, driver Dennis Bourne, Reg Eardley.

Brown Edge Jazz Band, late 1920s. We think taken in Basnett's garden with the Hollybush in background. Back: George Scarlett, Joe Dawson, Jack Rushton. Front centre Tom Basnett.

Alan Hayes supporting three of his cousins. Philip Worthy, David Mitcheson and Roy Mitcheson.

LEFT:
Brown Edge Judo Club 1967.
Tony Duka, ?, Phil Durber, ? Wooliscroft, John Clayton, Brian Durber, Martin Snape, ?, Fred Key.

Mums and babies pose outside Rock Cottage June 1943: Elsie Williams with Doreen, ?, Gladys Mountford with Brian, Chrissie Bourne with Margaret, ?, ? Schofield with Irene, ?, Charlotte (Lottie) Hewitt with Cedric (Cedric died of meningitis 1st May 1946).

Workingmen's Club 1970s.
Standing: ?, Derek Heath, ?, Bill Moseley, Horace Proctor, Tom Simcock, Dennis Wynne, Bill Simcock, Jim Mellor, Harry Hammond.
Seated: Gladys Hammond, Larry Abbott, David Knox, Rev A Moseley, Mannie Slater, ?.

BELOW:
Harry Worrall 1950s. This wooden garage stood opposite Thelma Avenue before Durbers and Walkers built their houses there.

Ray Adams 1968. Ray with his award for the 300lb bent-arm pull-over

Men at Work. About 1974 a group of local men got together to buy land belonging to Henridding Farm and formed Brown Edge Shooting Club. During the 1970s and 80s they frequently got in excess of 200 competitors. It was sold in 1986.
Kevin Powell, Alan Lowe, Ray Sutton, Bill Astbury, Keith Baker.

A day out to Trentham with the Workingmen's Club early 1950s.

The Hollybush darts team 1970s. Brian Banner, Roy Willis, Arthur Mayer, Phil Durber, Bert Harrison with grandson front, Dave Hargreaves.

Middle: The Brown Edge Workingmen's Club darts team. ?, Maurice Heath, Barry Hancock, Ken Mellor, Frank Scarlett, Harold Cartwright, Ron Sumner, ?, Dennis Wynne.

Bottom picture: The Hollybush Darts Team: ?, John Bowler, John James, Fred Proctor, Bob Durber, Paul Carroll, Jan Kapusta, John Salt, ?. An all Brown Edge final of Leek Charity Darts Competition. The Workingmen's Club beat the Hollybush 5-4.

The Hollybush Tug of War team in action on the Playing Fields 1970s. From the front: Bob Durber, Martin Snape, Arthur Pearson, Mick Hancock, Keith Brownsword, ? Grocott, Ivor Jones, Mick Rogers. Cheering them on at the left of the picture are front to back, Alan Snape, ?, Peter Snape.

The Hollybush Tug of War team after winning the local pub challenge 1970s. Keith Brownsword, Mick Rogers, Bob Durber, Martin Snape, Jim Porter, Mick Hancock, ?, Ian Rogers, Ivor Jones, Arthur Pearson.

Rose and Crown Tug of War team c1982. A team that won many trophies.

A day by the sea 1950s. Back: Eric Hargreaves, Derek Lear, Ron Stanway, Frank Harrison, ?. Front: Yvonne Miflin, ?.

Back: Graham Hudson, Bernard Sherratt, Bill Hulme, Geoff Thorley, Malcolm Shaw. Front: Phil Unwin, Roland Chadwick, Geoff Unwin, Dudley Frost, Robert Hudson, Alan Hudson (coach).

Cock of North Darts Team (*Leek Post and Times*) The Roebuck team who won the £150 first prize in the Watney Mann Open North of England Darts Championship at Stockport. Back: Bob Durber, Fred Proctor, Tony France, Ted Holdcroft, Ivor Challinor, Derek Berrisford. Front: John Hancock, Harold Cartwright, Fred Mountford, Maurice Heath, John Connell (licensee). Ted Holdcroft acquired the nickname 'cucumber' after steering the Roebuck to victory. In a nail-biting final against a team from Bolton Roebuck recovered from a 3-1 deficit to draw level. The win depended entirely on Mr Holdcroft. In his trilby hat he showed ice cool nerves to clinch the final game and was chaired aloft by his jubilant team mates.

RIGHT: National Indoor Catchweight Championship 1967. The Cheddleton Saxons Tug of War team beat Bosley Wood Treatment at Crystal Palace causing such an upset that letters were exchanged in the *Leek Post and Times*. Back: Bob Durber, Syd May, Graham Prime, Herbert Myatt, Basil Ball, Keith Tatton, John Salt. Front: George Buxton, Roy Woodward, Alan Robson.

RIGHT: Bob Chadwick, after winning the Alan Bradbury two-day competition at Leek. This was his first big senior win: Charlie Chadwick (dad), Stuart Biddulph, Bob, Brian Rourke, 1971. 1970 was a good year for Bob - he won the European Junior Championship, the British Junior Time Trial Championship and was second in the British Road Championship. As a professional he rode for Team Raleigh.

Rosamond Unwin: Scarlett's Nursery

The Scarlett family set up Woodside Nursery in the 1920s. George Scarlett, my grandfather, had been a jobbing gardener living in Turp's Row with his wife and children when the property in High Lane came up for sale. The house, 'Rosslyn', had been the old police house so was unusual in that it had a cell. The cell door had steel plating on both sides with a metal viewing hatch in the middle and a huge lock and key. On the inside it had an arched roof and a barred 'window'. It remained like this for many years.

The access to the nursery was off High Lane with the land extending up behind the Post Office to Cross Edge. The garden had two 80 foot greenhouses which had vines growing in them. A large Robin Hood boiler system heated them. Most of the land was used to grow plants to sell at market but there was also a cowshed, a potting shed, a pigsty and a small orchard where grandma kept hens. They employed people as and when they needed; my mother's uncle worked for them, as did Mr Grindy who lived nearby. The plant sales formed a large part of their income but they also sold vegetables direct from the garden. Grandma did a lot of the greenhouse work and the children - they had nine - were taught to make wreaths and took turns going to market with their father. Grandfather travelled to Hanley by horse and cart every Saturday, setting up his pitch on 'the stones' in the market square near to where the entrance to the Potteries Centre is now. Later, Tommy Rogers from Norton Green would transport the produce to and from Hanley or Burslem on his truck.

My grandfather was a well-respected show judge and travelled to places like Blackpool to judge as well as locally. After he died in 1942, Grandma tried to continue with some of the contract work and would travel on the bus to do the gardening at Leek High School. Later, she moved out of the house in High Lane to live with one of her daughters in Baddeley Edge but the property stayed in the Scarlett family - James (Dave Scarlett's dad) lived there. Later, some of the land was sold to the council and the retirement bungalows (Nursery Close) were built. The house was sold in 1994.

My mother, Mary Scarlett, was the seventh child of George and Mary Ann. She was born at Heaton's Villas in 1916. As a child she had pneumonia five times. She also had diphtheria and scarlet fever which meant staying in the Isolation Hospital in Tinster's Wood. For a while she was in service to Sir Francis Joseph and his family at The Hall in Alsager - her sister, Evie, worked there as a cook. Her sister, Lottie, worked for the Johnsons of Henshall Hall in Congleton. My mother loved it in Alsager but had to come back home when her father was taken ill. Before she was married she worked in Leeke's Grocery Store in Town Road, Hanley. She died in 1996 just short of her 80th birthday. She was a much loved mother of seven.

George Scarlett with his horse .

George Scarlett Snr going into his greenhouse. Stanley Scarlett sitting with his sister, Mary, holding Philip Barber about 1933.

The Workers: Sam Scarlett, Mr Grindy, Charlie Dawson, with George Scarlett behind.

George Scarlett Senr.

One of Harry Hammond's coaches.

Harry Hammond with his three wedding cars in the 1950s at the start of Quarry Lane, Lane Ends (now Church Road). A view of Top Heath Row in the background. Mr Hammond lived at High Lyn, Lane Ends and had a double garage off picture on the right. Gwenyth Hammond, Harry Hammond, Eric Hargreaves and Clarence Nixon.

Chatterley Whitfield Colliery looking north-east, August 1972.

Whitfield Middle Pit steps 1940s. Many thanks to Sid Boulton for helping to identify where this was taken. Harvey Durber is second row, 2nd from right.

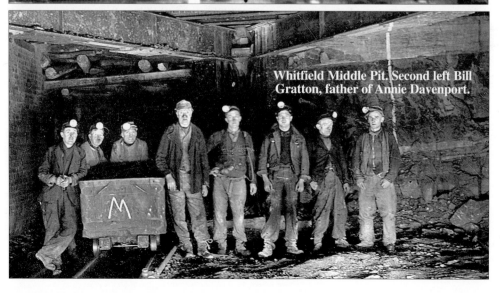

Whitfield Middle Pit. Second left Bill Gratton, father of Annie Davenport.

A group of retiring miners with their miniature Davy Lamps.
George Slack, ?, ?, ?, Arthur Simcock.

Arthur Lonsdale from High Lane, at Whitfield.

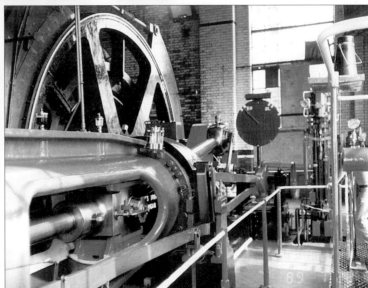

The Engine House at Whitfield Colliery, August 1972. The Worsley Mesnes winder (Hesketh Shaft), Cylinders 36 x 72 inches and drum 20ft.

Down the pit shaft. The launching of Chatterley Whitfield Mining Museum 24 May 1979.
?, ?, Derith Proctor, Ron Southern, ?.

Chatterley Whitfield August 1975. John Chadwick on the right.

John Chadwick, top and Overman Jackie Lloyd
outside the Institute Winder at Whitfield c1968.

A commissioned painting by artist Rob Pointon picturing the Friends of Chatterley Whitfield.
The painting is 3 metres long and 2 metres high and was exhibited in January 2009.
In the background are the head gears of Hesketh, Platt and Institute pits.

Burnfields Farm

William Thompson 1856-1928 of Burnfields Farm.	Selina Thompson 1867-1936 Burnfields Farm

BELOW:
May 1937 a bonfire on Marshes Hill to mark the Coronation of George VI and Queen Elizabeth. Dennis Frost, Joe Thompson and Bill Lowe. Dennis and Bill lived at Chapel Cottages, Hill Top and Joe farmed at Burnfields. The bonfire was built by these men with sleepers from Black Bull Station where Bill worked.

Shirley Hudson (nee Unwin): Burnfield's Farm

I was born at Burnfield's Farm and my parents were George and Gerty Unwin (nee Fradley). Dad's parents were Tom and Ginnie Unwin (nee Blakeman) and lived at Clay Lake Farm - now the Old Farmhouse. Burnfield's was 42 acres and it was enjoyable growing up there. Thompsons were there before us. I married Alan Hudson from Ladymoor Gate Farm in 1959. We lived at Broad Lane Cottage for a while but in 1971, when Mum and Dad retired, we took over the farm. We had pigs, hens and 45 Friesian cows. It was a difficult time in farming. When Joe Cumberlidge died in 1979 I took over his catering business with Eric Rowland and we became H & R Caterers. We were busy and after a lot of deliberation we decided to quit farming and sell up. Burnfields went for auction in 1998. The house was sold and the land was split up, and we moved to Endon where we now live.

Burnfields Farm looking down from Marshes Hill, May 1990.
Trade directories show Thomas Ainsworth 1900; Mr Thompson 1920.

Shirley Hudson (nee Unwin) and her sister Doreen c 1943.

Gerty Fradley with Joan Wilson, right and Hilda Lear (Simcock) c1925

Shirley's parents George and Gerty Unwin (nee Fradley) c 1940.

BELOW: July 1996, the cow sheds at Burnfields.
Graham Hudson (left) and Alan Hudson with some of their Friesian herd.

George Unwin, right with his brother, Stan and their first tractor and converted mowing machine (Fordson Major) early 1950s.

Yvonne and Dudley Frost at Burnfields Farm with the ducklings 1959.

George and Gerty Unwin at Broad Lane Cottage c 1973. They went to live at the cottage in 1971 when they left Burnfields.

Outside Burnfields Farm March 1954. David Beardmore, Doris (Doll) Tate, Ken Tate, Winnie Beardmore and Doreen Unwin.

Chris Hargreaves with Granny Margaret Hudson outside
milking machine shed at Newfold Farm.

Chris and Maggie Hargreaves with children, Newfold
Farm. Margaret, Ann, Chris, May, Maggie, Alan.

Newfold Farm

George Hargreaves, grandfather of Alan,
bought Newfold Farm some time in the
1920s for £1100. The 24 acres was farmed
afterwards by George's son, Chris, and
later grandson, Alan with his two sons,
Gary and Graham. Alan and his wife
Yvonne also had a daughter, Michelle.
They left the farm in 1993 and Tony Slater
bought the house and some land. The rest
was bought by David Jolley.

A christening at Singlet House
Farm with Harold
Shufflebottom, John and Beryl
Cook and Chris Hargreaves.

Newfold Farm. Silaging time.
Gary Hargreaves, Graham
Hargreaves, David Jolley
and Alan Hargreaves.

New Lane Farm

Sarah Sheldon (nee Buckley) wife of
Jessie c 1920.
Sarah and Jessie had three children,
Judith, Oliver and Spencer.

Three young men Oliver Sheldon,
Sidney Foster and Bill Bowyer c 1946.

Judith Sheldon (Hodgkinson) standing with Keith Hall and brother Spencer on
the horse at New Lane Farm, c 1936. Spencer died in 1937.

A one-horse
mowing machine at
New Lane Farm
c 1942.
Oliver Sheldon,
Eric Fox,
Judith Sheldon,
Derek Goodwin
and Frank Fox.

Singlet House Farm

William Durber with his prize shorthorn bull at Singlet House Farm.

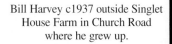

Bill Harvey c1937 outside Singlet
House Farm in Church Road
where he grew up.

ABOVE:
Jack Harvey centre
outside Singlet
House Farm c 1937.
His mother Lizzie
Harvey (nee
Durber) is on the
right. Jack's father
was William
Harvey. Bleak
house can be seen in
the background.

Hannah Durber on
a prize-winning
horse c 1903 at
Ladymoor Gate
Farm. Durbers later
moved to Singlet
House Farm.

A day out in the 1950s.
Peter Turner, Eric Hargreaves, Harold Cotterill, ?, Ivor Nixon, Frank Harrison, ?, Leonard Horton, Derek Lear, George Berrisford.

An outing from Keith's.

Bob Durber placing an insulator in a kiln at Bullers, Milton 1970s. Stan Mould is stooping and Don Rushton is driving the forklift.

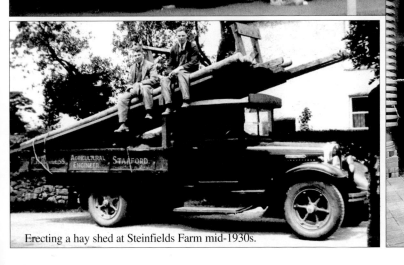

Erecting a hay shed at Steinfields Farm mid-1930s.

Margaret Ball (nee Bourne): Herbert James Bourne

Dad was born in Back Lane in 1913 and was one of 9 children. His parents were Frederick and Harriet Bourne (nee Mellor). In 1934/5 Grandad Bourne built Cliff House at Bank End from stone quarried on the site. Later Dad built a large garage on this land which his father had cleared. There is still a garage business on the site.

Dad went to Brown Edge School and when he left at 14 went to work in the mills at Leek. When he was courting my mother, Chrissie Clowes, who lived at Ipstones, on his way home he had an accident on his motorbike. He carried on driving but later he started bleeding from the ear. They took him to hospital and found he had a fractured skull. When he was lying in hospital, through the window he saw a coal man delivering and he thought 'I can do that' and that was how he came to start his business.

In 1937 he purchased a lorry and started fetching coal from the colliery and delivering it. He also drove for Browns' buses during the war. He married Mum in 1939 and they had two children, my brother Richard and I. My parents moved to High Lane, opposite Turner's garage. Dad later bought a removal van and then a wedding car and did taxis and weddings.

He was very active on the County Council for many years and was Chairman of Staffordshire Moorlands in 1972. In 1957 he moved to Willfield's Farm. He died in 1998 at Clewlows Bank, aged 84.

Herbert Bourne with his father, Frederick, outside the original Bank End Garage 1940.

Margaret Bourne (Ball) with her grandparents, Frederick and Harriet Bourne, at the rear of Cliff House, 1945. Frederick and his father (also Fred) built Cliff House in 1935 with stone quarried from the site, with the help of one assistant.

Herbert Bourne's coal lorry at Bank End Garage with Cliff House in the background.

Herbert Bourne: My memories of Brown Edge of 60 years ago (recorded in 1986).

In those days the population was about 850. Today it has reached 4,000 plus. From the Hollybush and the Long Row, at Sandy Lane, down High Lane to Annats Farm at Norton Green, there were only nine dwellings - three on one side, six on the other. These included two farms. The rest was open fields, hedges and trees. It was a common site to see grouse and snipe and to hear the sound of the corncrake in those fields.

As you can well imagine there was neither gas nor electricity, the only lighting coming from candles and oil lamps. However in the year 1930/31 electricity was connected from Stockton Brook - the first two poles being situated at the Lump of Coal and the Hollybush in Sandy Lane. It was gradually extended throughout the village. Where I lived at Bank End there was no water laid on, so all the villagers had to carry it from either the Sytch trough or the Spout near Hough Hill. There were only two telephones in the village.

A Bedford lorry of Herbert Bourne's at Marshes Hill c1940.

In those days there were very few cars, only two or three. People usually travelled by pony and trap, if they could afford; failing that, they walked. Trains ran from the Potteries via Stockton Brook and Endon and Leek. The local girls who worked in the Leek mills used the train. In 1921 Brown's Bus Co. of Tunstall introduced a service from Burslem to Brown Edge - the return fare was eight pence. The buses were charabancs with solid tyres and carbide lamps. The following year Mr Sam Turner introduced his bus service from Brown Edge to Hanley. Other local men, Mr Joe Horne, Mr Leigh Burgess and Mr George Mayer also ran buses.

A Bourne's removal van at Bank End. The house on the right is where Bakers live now. Herbert Bourne was now living in High Lane opposite Turner's garage.

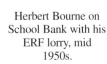

Herbert Bourne on School Bank with his ERF lorry, mid 1950s.

Joan Mountford: Berrisford's Shop

I was born in 1931 and my parents were Raymond and Nellie Berrisford (nee Fox). I have a brother George. When we lived at Endon Mother used to sell chips in Brown Edge, where the old Post Office was, and is now Helen Holdcroft's shop. Mother used to do the potatoes at home, drain off the water to carry them up from Endon and then re-fill with water from Sandy Lane well. She cooked the chips in two pans on a big unit over two coal fires. We moved to the shop in Sandy Lane, opposite the well, in 1935. It was a wet fish shop and greengrocers. Later we finished the greengrocers and just did fish and chips. Dad delivered wet fish. Mum then bought the house next door and made a supper room at the back of the shop. She had beetle drives there for both Church and Chapel and did tea and sandwiches. After Dad died Mum went to live in High Lane opposite Bratt's butchers. She died in 1986.

Nellie Berrisford (nee Fox) with her children Joan and George, c 1941.
Joan is wearing her stage dress she had for Sandy Lane Chapel.

Outside Berrisford's shop in Sandy Lane.
Joan Berrisford (Mountford), Brenda Harrison (Basnett), ?.

St Anne's Church, Joan Berrisford and Bill Mountford.

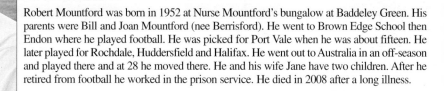

Robert Mountford was born in 1952 at Nurse Mountford's bungalow at Baddeley Green. His parents were Bill and Joan Mountford (nee Berrisford). He went to Brown Edge School then Endon where he played football. He was picked for Port Vale when he was about fifteen. He later played for Rochdale, Huddersfield and Halifax. He went out to Australia in an off-season and played there and at 28 he moved there. He and his wife Jane have two children. After he retired from football he worked in the prison service. He died in 2008 after a long illness.

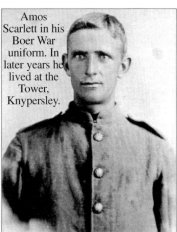

Amos Scarlett in his Boer War uniform. In later years he lived at the Tower, Knypersley.

First World War, taken at the school. Back: Major Dickinson, 7th Tom Baddeley.

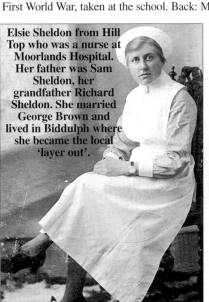

Elsie Sheldon from Hill Top who was a nurse at Moorlands Hospital. Her father was Sam Sheldon, her grandfather Richard Sheldon. She married George Brown and lived in Biddulph where she became the local 'layer out'.

Tom Chadwick, uncle to John Chadwick.

Bill Biddulph left, brother to Elsie Rowland. He served on submarines.

Arnold Lowe in army uniform c 1940. He married Mary Ann Berrisford and lived at Job's Pool.

Private Joseph Sheldon from Hill Top, born in 1896, one of five children of Sam and Hannah Sheldon. He was killed at Passchendale in 1917 aged 19.

Dennis Holdcroft was in the Welsh Guards. He married Jean Horne and they lived in Sandy Lane, later moving to a house on the Miners' Estate.

Burslem Police. Dan Tatton was a Police Special and is on the back row, 2nd right.

Bert Durber c1938 at the back of Dawson's shop in Sandy Lane. Bert married Lily Dawson. During the war he was in the Air Force.

Gladys Slack late 1930s. She was a nurse at the Isolation Hospital in Tinster's Wood. Gladys was born down Woodhouse Lane and married Albert Mountford. They had two children, Brian and Irene.

Bill Lowe, brother to Dorothy Simcock. After the army he joined the Police Force and was stationed in Stafford.

Auckland Horne was in the RAF. He was a wireless operator/air gunner. He grew up in Sandy Lane.

Left: George Scarlett was one of the boys who used to go to shorthand classes at the vicarage. He married May Smith.

An army boxing team. First left is Joseph Hancock, father of Alan Hancock. Joseph was killed at Dunkirk.

Leek Specials mid 1970s. John Chadwick, a Special for 28 years, is on the back row, first left.

James Scarlett, Auxiliary Fire Service. James was a chauffeur for Colonel Wade in Newcastle.

Alan Simcock was a Lance Bombadier with the Staffordshire Mercian Regiment and served in the far east.

Above
Eric Hargreaves, born in 1932 at 7 Heath's Row, Lane Ends, the third son (after Fred and Alan) of Fred and Lavinia Hargreaves. Mum died age 41 and Dad later married Nellie and they had three more sons, Roy, John and David. Eric was in the army 1952-1955 but two weeks after leaving the Suez Crisis came. He was re-called and married Dorothy Clements by special licence before leaving for Suez the next morning.

Edward Selby and his bride-to-be, Marjorie.   PC1981 Brian Simcock doing school duty in 1981.

The Brown Edge Over-Sixties Club

The club was formed in 1955. Founder members were Dr LE Garrett and Gladys Hammond. Members met every other Tuesday in the YMCA (TAB) in St Anne's Vale. Membership rose to over a hundred. Every year there was a birthday party to celebrate the founding of the club when a cake was cut by one or two of the oldest members. There were outings, June Fayres, an annual Harvest Service and Auction and a Christmas Party followed by entertainment and guest speakers. Every year there was an Easter Bonnet Parade and they had their own choir. When the TAB was demolished, members continued to meet in Sandy Lane Chapel. A small group of members still meet every fortnight in the Hollybush.

Over 60's Club Party in the TAB. Standing: ?, ?, Bill Warmsley, Charles Chadwick. Seated: Flo Hancock, Alice Rowland, Nellie Beardmore.

An outing on Turner's coach. Some of the travellers are Bill Rushton, Harry and Gladys Hammond, Mrs Pointon, Gordon Turner, Harriet Bourne, Martha Bailey, Jim Foster, Mrs Foster.

Bill Rushton cutting the anniversary cake c 1956. Standing: Harry Proctor, George Boulton, Mrs Garrett, J Hall, Jack Heath, Dr Garrett, Rev WT Attoe, ?, ?, Gladys Hammond, ?. Seated: ?, ?, Harriet Bourne, ?,Mrs Pointon.

Annual Harvest
Service and Auction.
Mrs Boulton,
Lily Tatton, Harry
Hammond, Bill
Basnett, Dan Tatton,
Gladys Hammond,
Bill Warmsley,
Jack Sherratt, ?.

Easter Bonnet Competition.
Standing: Jack Sherratt, ?,
Mrs Glover, ?, ?, Mrs Slack,
?, Fred Durber.
Seated: Charlotte Boulton, Gladys
Hammond, Doris Tyler,
Mrs Pickering, Mrs Stanyer.

Christmas Party.
Standing: ?, Ted Dutton,
Elsie Dono, Edgar Morris,
Mr Barnett.
Seated: Ivy Gethin,
Charlotte Boulton, Lily Tatton,
Mrs Dutton, Mrs Heath.

A presentation by Dan Tatton to Rev A Moseley on his transfer to another parish in 1985. Mrs Moseley is centre with their son, Christopher.

Carnival 1973.
Over 60's day out London to Brown Edge. John Lovatt, Mrs Glover, Mrs Pickering, Harry Hammond, Jack Sherratt.

BELOW:
Over 60s take a break in Torquay.

MOTHERS' UNION

A branch of the Mothers' Union commenced in about 1945.
Some of the founder members were Mrs Ramsden, Mrs Charles and Mrs Simmons. The group finished 4 years ago.

The Mothers' Union float 'The British Isles' won third prize in the Carnival 1973. The carnival was held at Willfield Farm. Dorothy Charles, Vera Cumberlidge, Gladys Hammond, Hilda Proctor, Alice Proctor.

Time for tea and cakes with The Mothers' Union, c 1970. Annie Shallcross, Beryl Cumberlidge, Mrs Simmons, Chrissie Bourne, Elizabeth Charles, Mrs Rastell and Dorothy Charles.

SCOUTS AND GUIDES According to Rev Lawton's book a Boy Scouts Club was tried in about 1935 but it only survived one or two seasons because the farmers complained of damage to their hedges and land by the scouts. In 1922 Miss M Lawton as captain and Miss Eva Proctor as lieutenant, after Investiture at Leek, became Girl Guide Officers. Mrs Horace Wardle, the County Commissioner, came to Brown Edge for the official enrolment of the First Brown Edge Company. A pack of Brownies was also formed with Mrs E Baddeley as Brown Owl. Mr Nixon and John Fenton ran a scout pack in the 1950s but there are no scouts in the village at present. However Guides and Brownies are run by Mandy Chell and Rainbows by Jackie Snape.

The Scouts form a Guard of Honour as Irene Mountford leaves Sandy Lane chapel, 1958
Lined up right: Dàvid Willis, Howard Ashman, Philip Gratton, Paul Carrol, Philip Worthy,
Philip Docksey. Lined up left: Gerard Carrol, ?, ?, Michael Tomkinson.
Centre are Judith Hewitt, Irene and Barbara Williams.

Brown Edge Cubs and officials in school hall c 1959. Back: Harry Bowyer, Robert Willis, Mrs
Heath, Gerard Carrol, May Fenton, Mrs Simmons, Rev RG Lansdale, George Hall, John Fenton.
Middle: 8th Peter Scragg, 9th Alan Simcock. Front: Noel Carrol, George Zurek, ?, Brian Redfern,
Terry Slater, Gerry Scragg, ?, Royston Turner, Robert Mountford. Margaret Wright in the chair

Miss Lawton,
Eva Proctor and Mrs
Baddeley.

Women's Institute

In 1921 a branch of the WI was formed with Mrs Lawton (the vicar's wife) as president. The two vice-presidents were Mrs Heath and Mrs Dickinson. The meetings were held in the Infants school. There is still a WI group on the village and they meet monthly in the school hall.

WI Late 1940s.
Standing: Mrs Hewitt, Ethel Dawson, ?, ?, Elsie Sims, Elsie Rowland.
Seated: Alma Proctor, Annie Mitchell, Nancy Harvey, Elsie Alcock.

WI Fashion Show.
Joyce Wedgwood, Betty Birkin, Gladys Bailey, Nora Rolinson, Gladys Lowe, Marjorie Twemlow, Betty Barker, Beatty Holdcroft.

WI in fancy dress c 1950.
Back: Beatty Holdcroft, Nancy Harvey, Annie Mitchell, Mrs Brown, Elsie Rowland, Margaret Tatton.
Front: Ivy Gethin, Gladys Bailey and Marjorie Twemlow as Tarzan's Jane.

British Legion Queen, Ann Morris c1942.
Back: ?, Manny Slater, Arthur Morris, Horace Hayes, ? Front: Lottie Hayes, ?, Ann, ?, Hilda Docksey.

WI Carnival Float 'Wales' late 1940s. Ethel Dawson, Marjorie Twemlow, Majorie Owen,
Mrs Brown, Elsie Alcock, Betty Egan, ?, Nancy Harvey, Kitty Clowes, Lilian Beckett, Elsie Rowland.

Endon Well Dressing celebrating Queen Victoria's Diamond Jubilee in 1897. The Brown Edge Band pose in front of the well. John Triner's grandfather, Richard Pointon, is second left, front row. He was 29.

Chatterley Whitfield Colliery had two bands. In addition to the Works' Band, composed mainly of mine workers, there was also the Junior Section seen here at practice under their conductor Mr Harry Machin.

An octet of cornetists! Terry Oates, Harry Machin Jnr, Keith Davenport,?, Colin Sherwin, ?, Dave Beardmore, Kenneth Tate.

Chris Tatton, Harry Machin, George Sheldon, Keith Davenport, Colin Sherwin, Harry Machin Snr, ?, Fred Woollams, ?, Malcolm Cox.

Harry Machin conducted the band for many years.

Harry Machin, Keith Davenport, Les Mason, ?, Colin Sherwin, Dave Kirkham, ?, Colin Dawson, Harry Machin Senr, Ken Tate, Alan Trotter, Dave Beardmore, Ken Bedson, Malcolm Cox, Jimmy Morris, Frank Machin, ?,Neil Micklewaite, ?, Ken Lambert, Michael Gidman.

Whitfield Band leading the procession by Endon Well, late 1940s.

The Horticultural Society

The WMC Chrysanthemum Society's Annual Show. Arthur Simcock, ?, Barry Simcock, Roy Barber, Arthur Morris, Tom Simcock, Bill Basnett.

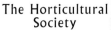

Arthur Simcock photographed by the *Sentinel* with his gigantic 3lb tomato. His greenhouse in the background.

Joe Berrisford and Frank Holdcroft.

The only double wedding at St Anne's Church, May 1959. On the left Majorie Ann Hudson of Ladymoor Gate Farm and Stanley Unwin, son of Mr and Mrs Thomas Unwin of Clay Lake Farm. Right: Alan Hudson (brother to Marjorie) from Ladymoor Gate Farm and Shirley Unwin from Burnfields Farm (niece of Stanley's). Shirley remembers she had her dress and veil from Huntbach's at a cost of £19 12s 6d. They had Harry Hammond's car and Joe Cumberlidge catered in the TAB for 2/6d a head. Shirley's mum and Alan's mum made sandwiches and took them in washing baskets for the evening do. After the wedding both couples lived at Burnfields Farm with Shirley's parents, Gerty and George Unwin. Six weeks later both newlyweds had a honeymoon weekend in New Brighton. Alan and Shirley have recently celebrated their Golden Wedding but sadly Marjorie died in 1974 age 35.

Wedding of George Unwin and Gerty Fradley, St Bartholomews, Norton, October 1938 (parents of Shirley and Doreen Unwin).

BELOW:
A double christening at St Anne's Church of David and Peter Cumberlidge c 1952.
Back: Arthur Brassington, Arthur Shallcross, Annie Shallcross, Rev WT Attoe, Vera Cumberlidge, Bob Cumberlidge, Iris Clarke, Leslie ?, Joe Cumberlidge holding Pam Cumberlidge. Philip Cumberlidge. Front: Shirley Brassington, Irene Shallcross, Kathleen Cumberlidge.

1944, the wedding of Jack Bailey and Gladys Bourne. Alma Proctor, George Bourne, Jack and Gladys, Joe Cumberlidge, Marjorie Roberts, Alice Cumberlidge.

1941, the Wedding of Dorothy Lowe and Joe Simcock, Endon Church. Francis Biddulph, Jim Simcock, Joan Morris, Bill Morris, Joe and Dorothy, Gertie Lowe, Bill Lowe, Beryl Foster.

1940s wedding of Harry Berrisford and Monica ?. Fred Berrisford, Charlotte Berrisford, Harry and Monica, Monica's dad.

Alma Foster and Robert Roberts in the 1940s. On the far right is Thelma Nicholls with George Foster next to her.

An Easter Wedding for Norah Baddeley and Arthur Garner 1953. Choir boys: John Hargreaves, John Crossley, Robert Bailey, David Crossley, John Fenton, John Foster, Frank Selby, Raymond Taylor.
Sunday Worshippers see Brown Edge Wedding (Leek Post and Times) Worshippers who attended Brown Edge Parish Church for Easter Sunday Morning Service found they were also attending a wedding. The couple who were married by Rev WT Attoe were regular members of the church. The marriage service was conducted followed by the communion service during which the bride and bridegroom, with their relatives, friends and other members of the congregation, were communicants. Rev Attoe said it was solemnised on Easter morning because the couple were such firm members of the church.

Wedding of Winnie Durber and Tom Baddeley.
Bill Downes, Tom and Winnie, Harry Durber, Ann Durber. Photo was taken at Singlet House.
Winnie and Tom lived at Woodside, St Anne's Vale for many years. They had one daughter, Norah.

Wedding of Evie
Scarlett and Reg Barber
c 1930.

Marjorie Green, Jim
Scarlett, Reg and Evie,
Ernest Heathcote and
Mrs Heathcote.

BELOW:
Stanley Scarlett and
Joan Rathbone.
Stanley and Joan met
at The Mount School
for the Deaf.

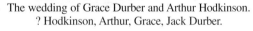
The wedding of Grace Durber and Arthur Hodkinson.
? Hodkinson, Arthur, Grace, Jack Durber.

Lewis Pointon and Pimsy
(Peggy) Sheldon 1944.
Lewis served in the Far East
and France in the war.
After the War Lewis set up
an electrical engineering
business in Nottinghamshire.
He lives in Selston, Notts.

The wedding of John Tatton and Joy Weaver. Toby ?, Glenda Weaver, Chris Tatton, Alice ?, Gladys Weaver, Dan Tatton, Lily Tatton, John and Joy, Melvin Weaver, Frank Weaver, Gladys Weaver, Yvonne Weaver, Laurence Weaver, Mrs Weaver, Heather Weaver, Clara Weaver, Charlie Weaver, Ivy Weaver, Norma Weaver, Dorothy Weaver.

LEFT:
Dan and Lily Tatton after their wedding in 1930. They were married at Burslem. Son, Chris, says this is the only known photo of the wedding day. The story goes that at Hixon their camera was accidentally dropped down the well in the garden. Lily wasn't very pleased.

Wedding of Gladys Tomkinson and Harry Hammond at St Anne's 16 July 1932. Gladys Joan Ellis, Vera Hammond, Bill Tomkinson, Harry and Gladys, Jack Hammond, May Tomkinson, Elsie Owen. Harry was from Baddeley Green.

1942 Wedding Group of Bill Harvey and Nancy Mountford outside Singlet House. Doris Harvey, Jack Harvey, Mary Baker, Harry Harvey, Bill and Nancy, Arthur Mountford, ?, Edith Mountford, Eileen Mountford, Enoch Mountford. Seated: Lizzie Harvey and Emma Mountford. Bill lived at Singlet House Farm and Nancy was from Cornhill.

April 27th 1946 St. Anne's Church. The wedding of Arthur Simcock and Hilda Lear. The vicar is Rev. EHB Richards. The bridesmaid on the right is Olwyn Lear (Durber)

BELOW:
Golden Wedding of Ginnie and Tom Unwin from Clay Lake Farm in the Tab c1957. They are pictured centre with their eight children, family and friends.

Above: Wedding at Endon Church of Joe Podmore and Evelyn Harvey late 1940s.
Back: Vera Biddulph, Elsie Rowland, Violet Higgins, George Harvey, Francis Brown, ?, Joe and Evelyn, ?, ?, ?, ?, Ginnie Proctor, ? Podmore, Ethel Biddulph, George Biddulph, ?, ?, Doris Podmore. Front: ?, ?, Janet Biddulph, John Biddulph. The bride, Evelyn, age 60 was marrying for the first time.

Left: 90th birthday of Elizabeth Emma Rowland, born October 1876, she died December 1966.
Standing: Elsie Rowland, Harry Heath, Millie Heath, Christine Woodward, Eric Rowland, Joan Rowland, John Rowland. Seated: Mrs Hall, Gladys Hammond, Elizabeth Emma, Harry Hammond, Alice Rowland, Robert Cope.

The wedding of John Fenton and May Tomkinson 1938. Murray Hollinshead, Vida Ellis, Joan Priestman, John and May, Bill Tomkinson, Elsie Owen.

Another St. Anne's
wedding 26 April 1942.
Syd Chadwick and Nellie Sims.
May Taylor, Mick Gibbon, Syd
& Nellie, Charles Chadwick,
Lucy Sims.
Front:
Frank Weaver
and Elsie Robbins.

25 October 1929
A wedding at Brown Edge
Church with Rev Lawton who
was vicar of St Anne's for 24
years 1920-1944.
Rev Lawton wrote and
published a history of the
church on its centenary in 1944.

Fred Smith, Elsie Preston,
James Henry Chadwick, Lily
Jolley (bride), Ethel Lancaster,
Harry Smith, Elsie Chadwick,
Rev Lawton.

The wedding group of
Harriet Hollins and
Arthur Williams. Alice
Hollins, ?, Arthur and
Harriet, Bill Hollins,
Winnie Hollins,
Norman Hollins, ?.
Harriet was a teacher at
St Anne's School.

May Durber and Jack Baddeley at the back
of Woodside, St Anne's Vale 1940s.
Front right Margaret Ibbs.
2nd row: ?, Jack, May, Brenda Durber,
Nora Baddeley.
3rd row: Harry Durber, ?, ?,
Dorothy Durber.

Charlotte Basnett and Reg Sutton c1914.
James W Basnett, ?, Charlotte, ?, Reg, ?,
James Basnett jnr. ?.
After James W Basnett died Bleak House
was split into two houses. Charlotte and
Reg lived in one half and James Jnr and
Florence lived in the other.

BELOW:
Wedding of Florrie Chadwick and Charles
Robbins. 1st left is Elsie Chadwick (Dono).

Sam Pointon and Edith Stonier Brown Edge August 1937.

Alan Pointon: Sam Pointon

Born in Sandy Lane on 25th June 1903 Sam's mum and dad were Maria and James. His mother died when he was five and he then went to live with his grandmother Bowyer in Norton Green. After Norton School his first job was with Heaton's Land Agents in Endon. Later he became a Storeman at Chatterley Whitfield Colliery rising to the management post of Storekeeper. In 1937 he married Edith Stonier, a teacher at St Anne's School. They set up home in Broad Lane where he lived until his death in 1957. He was closely associated with the church, a bellringer and chorister as well as a PCC member and Chairman of the Men's Society.

Too young to serve in the Great War and too old for the 2nd World War he joined the Whitfield battalion of Home Guard. I well remember the rifle kept behind the pantry door. Until his final years when illness forced him to use the bus he used to walk to and from work, 2 miles each way. During the hard winters, especially 1947 he 'hedged and ditched it' to quote from his own diary, and never missed a day's work. He loved his garden and went for long walks. Five or six miles on a Saturday afternoon was a regular event. He was a family man devoted to his wife and son.

RIGHT: Wedding of Alan Pointon and Ethel Sherratt.
Alice Holdcroft (Alan's sister), Frank Holdcroft, Alan and Ethel with Catherine Holdcroft in front. The book *A Brown Edge History* was written from Alan's meticulously recorded notes. He was born 1908 and loved his native village. He worked at Chatterley Whitfield as a mining surveyor and later a method study engineer. Both Ethel and Alan were members of Brown Edge Church, where Alan and his brothers were bell ringers. Alan died in 1981.

LEFT:
Wedding of Albert Willis and Vera Gratton January 15th 1944. Albert still has the bill for £45. (£7 dress, £4 priest, £12 10s flowers, £8 10s ale and stout, £1 10s Mrs Crossley and Band Room).

RIGHT:
Charles and Violet Chadwick (nee Dawson) on their Golden Wedding Day December 30th 1983.

The Wedding Day of William Henry (Harry) Davenport
and Annie Gratton 1939.

Berrisford - The Last Waltz
Joe and May Berrisford. May slipped on the dance floor at their
party at Bagnall Village Hall on the eve of their Golden Wedding
so for the actual day she was in hospital with a broken leg.

Golden Wedding of Sam and Minnie Sheldon (nee Harvey)
Sam died in 1999 and Minnie in 1998, both aged 86.

James Scarlett and Mabel Harrison 1939.
They had one son, David.